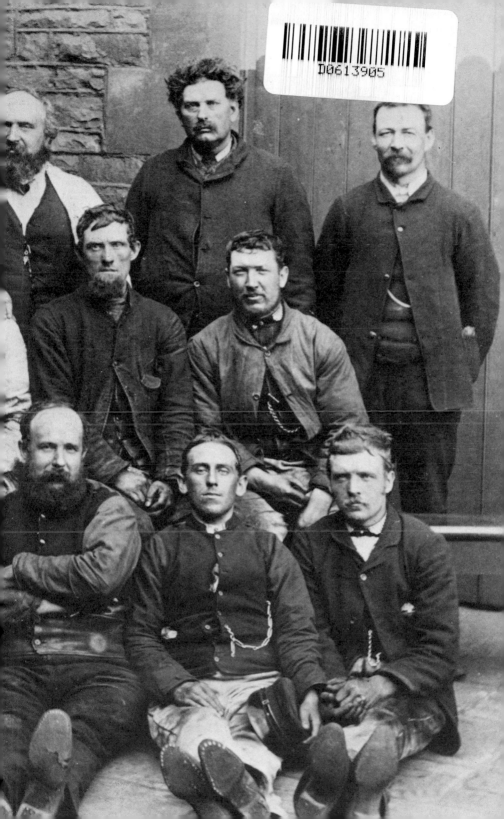

Grub, Water & Relief

By the same author

SIGNALMAN'S MORNING

SIGNALMAN'S TWILIGHT

GRUB, WATER & RELIEF

Tales of the Great Western
1835–1892

ADRIAN VAUGHAN

John Murray

© Adrian Vaughan 1985
First published 1985
by John Murray (Publishers) Ltd
50 Albemarle Street, London w1x 4bd

Typeset by Inforum Ltd, Portsmouth
Printed and bound in Great Britain
by The Pitman Press, Bath

British Library Cataloguing in Publication Data
Vaughan, Adrian
Grub, water & relief : tales of the Great
Western 1835–1892.
1. Great Western Railway—History—
19th century
I. Title
385'.0942   HE3020.G8
ISBN 0–7195–4176–X

To the known and unknown heroes
of the nineteenth-century Great Western Railway
and especially in memory of the pair
of Irishmen who danced on Daniel Gooch's hat

AUTHOR'S NOTE ON THE TITLE

In 1963 I spent a week firing to Driver Kingdom of Oxford shed working the 9.15 p.m. fish from Oxford to Basingstoke with a 'West Country' class pacific, returning with an ex-LMS 2–8–0 on the 2 a.m. freight for Oxley. We arrived back in Oxford between 4 and 4.30 each morning where we were relieved by a 'Brummy' crew. On the Friday morning we were feeling decidedly frayed around the edges so that when the relieving crew came swarming up the cab steps onto the footplate, Don and I lost little time in civilities but hastened down the opposite steps. As we clambered down with our bags and coats I heard the Brummagem driver exclaim, with considerable sarcasm in his voice, 'Gow-on then, booger off – that's all yow Western men think about – Grub, Water and Relief!'

CONTENTS

ILLUSTRATIONS

Between pages 84 and 85

ACKNOWLEDGEMENTS AND LIST OF SOURCES

I wish to thank the many expert historians, library staff and others who helped me with the large amount of research necessary to write and illustrate this book: Robert J. Excell and A. Hall-Patch, Science Museum, London; Mike Rutherford, National Railway Museum, York; Miss J. Coburn, GLC Record Office; Nick Coney, Public Record Office, Kew; the staff of the Newspaper Library, Colindale; G. D. Norris, Library of the Royal Engineers, Chatham; A. C. Hendricks, Ordnance Survey, Southampton; Miss J. Colwell, Tredegar Library; John Chandler, Trowbridge Library; Roger Trahearne, Swindon Library; M. K. Stammers, Liverpool Maritime Museum; A. W. H. Pearsall, National Maritime Museum, Greenwich; Tony Conder, British Waterways Museum, Stoke Bruerne; Mrs H. A. McTiffin, Windsor Library; the office staff of the *Windsor & Eton Gazette*; Tim Bryan, GWR Museum, Swindon; Chris Tagholm, Public Relations Officer, BRWR; Roger Penhallurick, Royal Institution of Cornwall; Miss Yoxall, Abingdon Museum; Laurence Waters; Sue Joslin and Alan Brock, British Rail/OPC Joint Venture; Dr R. W. White, who supplied valuable information about the engine-house at West Drayton, and Chris Turner, who introduced me to him; Kelvin White, Alan Garner and Eddy Brown, Broad Gauge Model Railway Society. I must also thank my friend Sean Bolan for help with vital addresses and sources of illustrations; Duncan McAra and Jeannie Brooke Barnett at John Murray for their many kindnesses; my sister, Frances, provided 'B & B' in her house conveniently close to the Public Record Office, Kew; my friends from steam days at Challow, Ron and Jo Price, who regularly provided me with a generous second home when I was working at Colindale; and my family – Susan, Rebecca and Constance – were remarkably cheerful in accepting the necessity of getting up at five o'clock on several mornings to drive to Norwich station for the early train to London.

The information for this book was drawn largely from the huge

collection of Great Western Railway official books and papers held at
the Public Record Office, Kew, and also from the Great Western
Railway staff magazine, from *The Times* and other newspapers held at
the British Library's newspaper library at Colindale. Also consulted
was Henry Ralph's reminiscences of his fifty years' work at Reading
station, printed as a pamphlet and held at the Central Reference
Library, Reading; Charles Babbage's book, *The Life of a Philosopher*,
published by Longman in 1864; and articles in the magazine *Temple
Bar* for January/April 1884 and May/August 1892. For the story of
Tom Plowman's trip to London I am indebted to *A Cotswold Village* by
J. Arthur Gibbs, published by John Murray in 1909.

ONE

The Great Western at Sea

In 1825 George Stephenson was mapping-out the route of his Liverpool & Manchester Railway, a forty-mile line without a hill in sight yet beset by one enormous obstacle – the 'uncrossable' Chat Moss, as formidable a barrier across the western approaches to Manchester as any mountain range. To venture onto this wilderness of reeds and quaking ground without a local guide was to court death so George rode to the lonely Moss village of Astley Green, dismounted at the cottage nearest the marsh and knocked at the door. It was opened by John Hurst, weaver. In the room behind, his son James looked up from a loom but his wife continued to treadle her spinning wheel and watched the stranger covertly.

'My name is Stephenson,' said George. 'I need a guide for the Moss while I'm surveying the line of the new railroad. Will you come with me? I'll pay you and the lad five shillings a day between you.'

Father and son knew the Moss well and leaped at the chance to earn so much money, so easily and in such distinguished service, for they had heard of the new railway, and the suggestion that the Moss could be crossed by any road had been the talk of the village for weeks. John and Jim Hurst thought it could not be done but for five shillings a day they were more than willing to leave their looms and walk the Moss with the Chief Engineer of such an astonishing scheme. Jim acted as guide, with his father carrying surveying equipment and for days they worked their way across the swamp, Jim probing the squelchy depths for a path, Stephenson's life in his hands.

When the survey had been completed successfully John Hurst had earned more in days than he would have got in weeks on the loom and Jim had earned Stephenson's admiration and a promise. 'I'll mek a railwayman o' thee when thee gets old enough.'

When it came time to build the railroad John Hurst was given a contract to recruit local labour and create some of the drainage necessary and Jim worked in his father's gang. For all the men it was a blessing and for Jim it was a near-miraculous escape. He had never been to school and could neither read nor write but since the age of five had helped his parents weave. Without the railway he would have continued hopelessly at the loom until the workhouse, the army or the mill claimed him – and many a proud weaver had chosen the army, with its brutal discipline, in preference to becoming a machine minder in a cotton mill. The years of unpaid, hungry toil during what ought to have been a childhood had given his character an under-standable hardness: his long, bulb-ended nose like an angry exclamation mark and his aggressively bulging eyes seemed well suited to his quick temper and jealous manner. Certainly he did not suffer fools gladly but he had an attractive side to his nature, he was a loyal friend and a hard worker, full of confidence in himself and his future and had no difficulty in courting a local lass of sixteen, a year younger than himself. They were married in 1828 and a year later she gave birth to their first son, Edward, who would one day also become a driver on the Great Western Railway. In 1830, when the Liverpool & Manchester Railway opened, George Stephenson saw that Jim was taken on as a cleaner in Salford engine house under the supervision of the Foreman, an elderly Scotsman called Sandy Fife. Jim was made a fireman in 1832 and two years later he crossed the footplate to become a driver.

Life was good. Far from being a redundant hand-worker at a medieval craft he was now one of a very small group of men whose services were in the greatest demand; he was among the highest paid workmen in Britain; the eyes of the scientific world

were upon the engines he drove; engineers rode his footplate
and sometimes even asked his opinion on technical matters. He
had also a band of lay admirers – early 'loco-spotters' – whose
devotion to the iron horse he rewarded and fostered by giving
the occasional footplate ride or by allowing them to ride when
they jumped up behind on his tender and rode precariously
through the country on the buffers.

Several of the engines which Jim drove were built at the
Vulcan works of Charles Tayleur & Co beside the Warrington
branch of the Liverpool & Manchester Railway. There were
close ties between the works staff and the L & M men – some
had worked for both concerns. Often men from Vulcan drove a
new or overhauled engine to the L & M shed at Salford or rode
an L & M footplate to bring a 'cripple' engine back to the works
so it was natural that the works' apprentices should ride with
Jim Hurst and be well known to him. One of these was a
seventeen year old – Daniel Gooch.

Dan Gooch was a gentleman railwayman. A few years before
1834 the lives of Gooch and Hurst would never have crossed but
in the new world of railway engineering ability rather than
'breeding' mattered. Gooch was born into engineering at
Bedlington, Northumberland, on 25 August 1816, the third son
of John Gooch, manager of an iron foundry. Dan grew up
among machinery and molten iron at his father's works and also
knew something about mining from visits to his uncle who
managed a nearby colliery. George Stephenson frequently
came to the Bedlington works on business and was a personal
friend of John Gooch – so Jim Hurst and Dan Gooch, despite
their different backgrounds, had a friend in common.

At the age of fifteen Gooch started his apprenticeship in the
locomotive works of Robert Stephenson in Newcastle upon
Tyne but a year later his father took a managerial post in the
Tredegar ironworks of Samuel Homfray and Dan went with
him. Tredegar was a strange place to go, voluntarily, in 1832.
Utterly remote at the head of the Sirhowy valley in Monmouthshire the town was a man-made hell. Men and children worked

killing hours in the smoke and filth of the foundries and were maimed by molten metal. Their only medical help was that administered by the 'Penny Doctor'. Wages were paid in Homfray's private coinage – banks were not allowed in the town – so workers spent their coins in Homfray's shops, buying food at Homfray's prices. Poverty and malnutrition followed and disease followed both.

Father and son arrived in the town just as its first cholera epidemic had started; they were strong, well fed and healthy and survived for eighteen months until just before Christmas 1833, John Gooch caught the plague and died on Christmas Day. Dan left Tredegar at once and spent a miserable Christmas with his mother in Warwick before going north, in January 1834, to the Vulcan works of Charles Tayleur. He took no relaxation from his apprenticeship or from the study of science as it applied to locomotive design. No one but Dan was going to help Dan succeed and to spend time and money in entertainments would have been a waste – the nearest thing to relaxation he got was his footplate riding with Jim Hurst. Drawn by their common interest in steam engines they became good friends. Dan was quiet and thoughtful and could never annoy the excitable, impetuous Jim – indeed, Jim loved to answer his questions; they learned from each other and Jim, five years older than Dan, became a kind of big brother to him and many a fine 'spin' they enjoyed together across the Moss within sight of the weavers' cottages at Astley Green. But his enthusiasm for hard work got the better of him after eight months at Vulcan; perhaps, too, his health had been affected by his contact with cholera. In August 1834 he became seriously ill and was forced to retire to his mother's house at Warwick. Charles Tayleur sacked him after a week.

He did not recover his health until Christmas and in January 1835 went to work in a foundry in Dundee where ships' engines were made. Twelve months later he was back in Newcastle, at Robert Stephenson's works, as a draughtsman charged with the design of two 6-ft gauge engines for a railway in New Orleans.

He was delighted with this broad gauge – there was more room under the boiler in which to arrange the machinery, to have larger bearings, bigger boilers and cylinders – enabling the engines to be more stable on the track at speed. The concept was big – Gooch liked that – he saw no reason why the new, powered transport should follow the gauge of horse-drawn carts – the 'coal-cart' gauge, he called it contemptuously. When George Stephenson had laid out the Stockton & Darlington Railway it was intended to carry coal as a turnpike road carried goods – anyone could use the way on payment of a toll and to ensure that as many carts as possible could run on the railroad Stephenson had measured the distance between the wheels of one hundred carts in the area, made an average and decided that that would be the width between his rails. Thus he arrived at the 'standard' gauge for railways: 4 ft 8½ in.

Gooch designed the two 6-ft gauge engines and their construction was under way when, in October 1836, a man called Robert Hawkes offered him the job of Works Manager in a locomotive factory which Hawkes proposed to build at Gateshead. Gooch was only twenty but in high standing among the locomotive fraternity of Newcastle, and his ambition was eager for the grand design. He left Robert Stephenson without a qualm and threw himself into the new job. As the new factory was no more than a wish in the mind of Hawkes, Gooch could do nothing in Gateshead so he set out by stage-coach for the south, to find Isambard Kingdom Brunel, the thirty-year-old Engineer of the 7-ft gauge Great Western Railway, founded in August 1835, and to canvas from him orders for broad-gauge engines. Brunel's life at that time may be described as nomadic. He insisted on being in charge of every detail of design and construction on 118 miles of railway, every station, lamppost and a score of great marvels of engineering beside, travelling as fast as horseflesh could carry him, sleeping four hours in twenty-four, sometimes at a country inn, sometimes in his specially built carriage, the 'Flying Hearse', as it bounced along rutted roads from one site to the next. Lacking any kind of electric communications no one could be sure where Brunel was until he arrived. Gooch was no laggard but in a ten-day chase across six counties he never caught up with Brunel and returned to Gateshead bereft of orders but thoroughly impressed by the magnificent scale of the quarter-built Great Western and more certain than ever of the correctness of the broad gauge.

Back at Gateshead, having used up what money he had on the hire of horses, turnpike tolls and stage-coach fares, he found that Hawkes had gone bankrupt, the factory would thus not be built and he, Gooch, was out of a job and broke. But the railway was then, as always, a family affair and his elder brother Tom, an engineer on the Manchester & Leeds Railway, rescued him with a job in the M & L R offices; Dan was safe from starvation, indeed, he had a secure job but he could not remain content with his position. He was restless with the puny little coal-cart gauge engines, he had seen the possibilities and wanted to work on the grand – the broad gauge – scale.

Jim Hurst was very pleased to be driving 4 ft 8½ in.-gauge engines. He had had no education but he was learning to read and write and was earning more than, say, a solicitor's clerk. He had the status of a public figure, well known to the thousands who used the Liverpool & Manchester line and a reputation for speed and arbitrary behaviour which would have been the envy of any stage-coach driver. But long hours at work and a cavalier attitude towards safety was a dangerous combination and in May 1837, after he had caused a collision, Jim was sacked.

In July 1837 Gooch heard that Brunel was looking for a Locomotive Superintendent and on the 18th wrote, applying for the job. The letter he wrote* was a model for those wishing to put the best possible gloss on their previous experience but in any case Gooch's ability, character and enthusiasm for the broad gauge were well known to Brunel who recommended his Directors to employ Gooch without delay – without even the formality of an interview. The Directors handed the responsi-

* See Appendix 1.

bility back to Brunel and a few days later, when Brunel was at Tayleur's works to see the engines which were being built there for the Great Western, he went across to Manchester to meet Gooch for the first time. He enlisted him immediately as Locomotive Superintendent of the Great Western Railway.

Gooch was not quite twenty-one years old yet his experience was immediately useful to Brunel whose otherwise infallible engineering instinct always seemed to fail him when he had to deal with locomotives. Gooch was uncomfortably aware of the poor quality of Tayleur's engines and the even lower standard of Mather Dixon, Brunel's other locomotive supplier. He also knew that the pair of 6-ft-gauge engines he had designed for New Orleans were still at Robert Stephenson's works because the American firm had gone bankrupt and he urged Brunel to buy them both – they were strongly made, he knew they were well designed and could easily be altered to run on the Great Western's 7-ft gauge. Brunel did as Gooch suggested and bought the engines, the first of a long line of highly successful machines. Their names, beautifully evocative, started the Great Western tradition for naming classes of engine with a class name – indeed, no GWR broad-gauge engine was ever numbered* – and though other companies sometimes copied the style none ever achieved the brilliance of Gooch's original inspiration – the 'Stars': *North Star, Morning Star* and the rest.

Gooch also knew where to find enginemen and before he left for West Drayton, Middlesex, to be the temporary headquarters of the Great Western's locomotive department, he recruited twenty enginemen, drivers and firemen, including 'Wor Bill' Thompson, Michael John Almond, John Liver, Harry Appleby of Newcastle and his old mentor, Jim Hurst. Gooch did not know that Jim had been unemployed for thirteen weeks until he contacted Sandy Fife and between them they contrived a surprise for him. Sandy sent a note to Jim's home,

---

* Except standard-gauge engines temporarily converted to run on broadgauge track and engines taken over from other broad-gauge companies.

summoning him to Salford shed and when he presented himself the old Scot said, 'Jamie, I've a choice o' four jobs for ye. America, Spain, Russia or the Great Western.' The last, being the only one in reach of home was the obvious choice. 'Aye,' replied Sandy solemnly, 'then be at ma' hoose th'nicht – your new Superintendent will be wanting to interview ye.'

Jim walked into Sandy's front parlour that evening, all keyed up for an examination by the Locomotive Superintendent of the Great Western Railway and was astonished to find himself face to face with young Dan Gooch, grinning broadly, his hand outstretched in welcome. They talked of their footplating days together before Gooch asked him if he would be willing to move south as a driver on the Great Western and if he would mind going by sea, in charge of the Tayleur engine *Vulcan* he would eventually be driving and one other, *Premier,* from Mather Dixon. Jim accepted at once and Gooch recognising that Jim had been out of work for months told him he could start in the morning at Tayleur's works as the Great Western's representative at the construction of *Vulcan*. His wages were to be 6s 8d a day.

When *Vulcan* was completed it was given a trial run and then taken in pieces – wheels and frames as one, boiler with chimney dismounted – to the Sankey canal and loaded into a barge which was then hauled by teams of men down to Widnes dock, junction for the Mersey where the bargee hoisted sail for the thirty-odd-mile journey down to Liverpool dock. *Vulcan* was hoisted piecemeal onto the deck of a paddle-steamer to join *Premier* for the passage to London. It was, the sailors said, a fast passage – six days port to port – but it was six days too long for Jim and the deck still seemed to heave even when the ship was tied up on the river side of the Regent's canal basin amidst the forestry of the world's shipping, just west of the Isle of Dogs. The steamer was too big to pass the lock into the basin and its paddles prevented it from lying close alongside the quay so it is probable that the larger pieces of locomotive, each weighing 7 tons or so, were lowered into a barge lying in the river directly below the ship's cranes. Both engines fitted easily into one barge, their spare parts went into another. The little fleet then passed the lock, through the basin and into the canal for a trip through Shoreditch and St Pancras to the Paddington arm of the Grand Junction canal and, eventually, to West Drayton.

While the Great Western's locomotive fleet was still at sea the Great Western Directors received a letter of complaint from the Directors of the Liverpool & Manchester Railway and the Manchester & Leeds Railway which accused Brunel of 'offering inducements to our enginemen to go to work on your railway'. Not only was this a form of piracy, they wrote, but it was also likely to set a very dangerous precedent because 'competition in wages among Companies is giving the men a sense of their own importance so that those left behind want to strike for higher wages'. The letter concluded with the suggestion that employers ought to combine to create a national, maximum wage.

The Great Western Board was flustered at this and called Brunel from such trivial matters as excavating Box tunnel to answer the complaint. He trekked in the hundred miles on horseback and pointed out to his Directors that the enginemen were indeed men of importance to any railway, declared that he saw nothing wrong in offering such men a higher wage as an inducement to move south and concluded, 'I will just observe that it would be most improper of us to set the men such an example as combination as we could hardly complain if they were then to combine in an agreement as to what they consider to be a national minimum wage.' Brunel's fairness won the day, the Directors were soothed by the rational words, ceased to be flustered and allowed the great man to go back to the problem of tunnelling nearly two miles through Box hill.

When Gooch arrived at West Drayton he found a lonely scattering of houses around a rectangular green with the de Burgh's mansion and the parish church in the south-west corner and the Uxbridge/Colnbrook road passing through north to south. Hounslow Heath of villainous repute lay for miles to the east while the several, straggling streams of the river

Wrayisbury, flowing north/south, formed the western boundary. At the north end of the village street the road passed through the Great Western embankment under an arch of white brick. The de Burgh Arms public house was a few yards north of the bridge and just beyond that the Grand Junction canal swung away to the north under a hump-backed bridge. On the embankment, immediately west of the white arch, was the railway station.

Gooch rented a cottage, hired a horse and set to work for his, as yet, locomotiveless railway. He ordered an office to be built in the village for his gestating department, supervised the erection of temporary coke ovens and engine house, badgered the Directors for otherwise non-existent machine tools – which he knew only too well he was going to need – and worked out how to get *Vulcan* and *Premier*, weighing 16½ and 13½ tons respectively, out of their barge, onto the high embankment and into the engine house one mile from the canal. There was no crane at West Drayton's rural wharf strong enough to lift the engine parts but, by the greatest good fortune, 400 yds west of the wharf, 400 yds closer to the engine house, a massive old elm tree was growing on the canal bank with one sturdy branch projecting over the water and Gooch decided to use this as a support for his lifting chains and pulley. When the barges arrived and tied tight against the canal bank, rails were placed 'ship to shore', the wheels/frame of each engine was hoisted onto the rails and then rolled off onto iron plates, the boilers were hoisted onto special trolleys and run onto the bank where temporary sheer legs were erected to hoist them up onto their wheels. A team of horses was attached and each engine rumbled over it. They were pulled up the long slope of the station approach to a temporary track along the embankment to the engine house situated on the north side of the line at what is now the 14¼ mile post where the high embankment gives way to shallow cutting where it was easy to level out a space on the hillside. When the engines were safely stowed into their simple shed – open to the elements on the south side but with a brick wall to the north, 132 ft x 20 ft under a pitched roof – having 'put the engines to bed' for the first time, Gooch invited Jim Hurst back to his cottage and for several weeks the two friends shared the cottage and the work.

Shortly before Christmas 1837 Brunel received enough rails and timbers to lay one and a half miles of his carefully thought-out track from the engine shed to Dog Kennel bridge one mile east of Langley station. Brunel was the first man to give real thought to track design, to consider the need for high speed and silent running and the result was very different from the crudities of Stephenson's method. Unfortunately for Brunel, George Stephenson was first in the field, the public and press had decided that it could neither be improved upon – except by Stephenson – nor contradicted, so Brunel had to contend with a great deal of ill-informed abuse. He was accused of being 'extravagant', of wasting his shareholders' money in novelties merely to draw attention to himself. John Hawkshaw, Engineer of the Manchester & Leeds Railway, said, 'The mode of laying the [broad gauge] track is attempting to do in as difficult and expensive a manner that which can be done at least as well in a simple, more economic manner.' Hawkshaw had a cheek! His rails, laid by the Stephenson method, rested on stone blocks without cross-ties to keep them to gauge; the heavy blocks were buried in the ground, frequently subsided and were extremely difficult to realign and the rails, bridging the space between each block, often broke under the weight of a train. Hawkshaw's track was not even suitable for coal-carts let alone express trains. Brunel gave his rails continuous support, laying them along heavy baulks of timber called longitudinals which were held to gauge by cross-ties called transoms and which were bolted down to telegraph pole-sized wooden piles driven 15 ft into the ground. It took working experience to show up the uselessness of the piles but Brunel's was the first attempt at making a railroad in keeping with the potential power of steam.

George Stephenson was never rude about Brunel's track and, indeed, the two men were on the best of terms. They were travelling in a train one day and Stephenson was wearing his famous plaid, famous for its tight fit, the result of Stephenson's secret and intricate method of folding it about his body. Brunel, sitting opposite, studied the folds until Stephenson said, 'I see you are studying my plaid. I will wager you ten pounds you cannot put it on correctly.'

'Ten pounds against the plaid,' replied Brunel. 'When we get out at our station I will put the plaid on immediately and if I wrap it correctly I will keep it – otherwise I will pay you ten pounds.' At the end of the journey Stephenson unwound the plaid and handed it to Brunel who carefully wrapped it around himself with perfect folding. He had worked out the system sitting in the train and Stephenson's final unwrapping had confirmed the method in Brunel's quick brain.

On 28 December 1837, with one and a half miles of track laid from the engine shed westwards, Gooch was able to give his fleet, *Vulcan* and *Premier,* a trial run. They were very poor tools, badly made to a design that can only be called 'freakish' – though they looked impressive with their wide-set stance and huge driving wheels: *Vulcan* had a single pair of 8 ft diameter wheels, *Premier* a 7 ft pair while contemporary standard gauge engines' driving wheels were only 5 ft or 5 ft 6 in. diameter. Brunel wanted a high track speed with a low piston speed and a mere 10½ tons total weight – speed for the public with minimal wear and tear on locomotive and track, an excellent ideal but one which led to almost useless engines being built. Brunel left the actual design to the locomotive builders and to keep the engines' weight down they made boilers and cylinders which were far too small while the driving wheels they made enormous in order to comply with Brunel's desire for a low piston speed. This was altogether the worst possible combination for a loco-motive and to make matters even worse there was no room inside the tiny boilers to distance sufficiently the steam collect-ing pipe from the surface of the boiling water so that water was carried with steam into the cylinders – an effect known as priming – which could burst the cast-iron cylinders or bend a connecting rod because water is incompressible and has to go somewhere if it is trapped in a cylinder by the moving piston.

Jim Hurst took the lead with *Vulcan*, Gooch riding with him into the new era, with Brunel and some Directors riding behind on *Premier*. The engines had some difficulty in negotiating the points out of the shed onto the main line and de-railed, but once onto plain track managed to wheeze along under a shower of hot water from their tall chimncys. The Directors were unaware that anything was wrong, indeed, they were very excited about their trip and Gooch felt he could not criticise his Chief's engines when no one was asking his opinion but he, Jim Hurst and John Liver, the driver of *Premier*, were gloomy when they finally got their puny charges back inside the shed. The many bystanders were impressed and that evening in the de Burgh Arms the villagers and railway workmen with some navvies held a seasonal party to celebrate the great event. Gooch was invited along with his men.

Gooch hated parties and this one, as a celebration of loco-motive feats, was rather premature but he went along because Jim and John Liver wanted him to go. He was the last to arrive and found the pub in full spate, singing was thundering out into the night and there was not a hat or coat-peg onto which to hang his top hat so he put hat and coat on the floor in a corner and elbowed his way through the crowded bar to find Hurst and Liver. They, like Gooch, had no small talk – if Jim had been a chatterer he would not have been invited to lodge with Gooch – and the entire Locomotive Department of the Great Western Railway went into a huddle in a corner of the room to discuss locomotives and the difficulties to come. Behind them the beer and brandy flowed freely and soon the English and Scots con-tingent of navvies were calling for 'Three cheers for Mr Gooch.' Gooch managed to ignore them. Then two Irish navvies stepped up and asked if Mr Gooch would do them the honour of joining in a reel. Gooch declined the honour and went back to his technical discussion.

Two minutes later the Irish gentlemen were back and, to

Gooch's amazement, were carrying his top hat. 'Ye won't mind if we have yer hat fer a stand-in?' they asked, as they put it down on the floor. A space appeared around them, a tin whistle struck up its bubbling tune and the inebriated navvies began to dance. Gooch and his small crew had their backs to the bar, facing the dancers and the small, tight semicircle beyond them. Few others were aware of what was happening and went on with their noisy drinking, those close by either cheered the dancers on, clapping out the time, or glowered sourly and looked at Gooch to see if he was going to make a fight of it. Jim Hurst was raring to dive in and rescue the topper but Gooch was against it, saying he would rather lose his hat than his life. The dancing navvies were unexpectedly light on their feet, quick, darting steps nudged the hat this way and that until, when tension had been screwed up tight a boot came down square on the topper's crown, squashing it flat. The dance stopped abruptly, Gooch dived forward, flanked by Hurst and Liver, grabbed up the remains of his hat, and with the other two snatched coats from the floor or pegs and bored their way out into the darkness. Gooch, seething with rage and hurt pride, strode home with Jim Hurst almost trotting to keep up, cursing the momentary weakness that led him to join a navvies' celebration.

TWO

Navvies versus Cavalry

On 22 March 1838 Daniel Gooch married Miss Margaret Tanner in Bishop Wearmouth. Gooch determined, from the start of his marriage, never to get into debt 'which is so destructive of peace of mind' and adopted a plan of 'saving something every week – even if it is only a pound'. His 'only' sounds oddly naive considering that most men at that time were getting only a pound a week on the railway while the drivers, the best paid men, such as Jim Hurst got £2 7s 6d out of which he paid 6s a week for his cottage at Paddington. The excitement of getting married laid the new Mrs Gooch low and the honeymoon consisted of seven days at her parents' house while she rested, preparing for the gruelling, thirty-six-hour stage-coach journey to London. They arrived in the metropolis after thirty changes of horses, she was prostrated for over four months and Dan Gooch took refuge in the locomotive problems at West Drayton.

He had eight lame engines on the shed while the only reliable machine, *North Star,* was marooned miles from the rails at Maidenhead. *Premier* and *Ariel* from Mather Dixon were poorly constructed and prone to derailment. The Tayleur engines – *Vulcan, Aeolus, Bacchus, Apollo* and *Neptune* – were better made but all of them were far too small in their boilers and far too large in their driving wheels. The eighth engine, *Thunderer,* which had arrived while Gooch was away getting married, was an imaginative attempt by the Newcastle firm of R. W. Hawthorn and their designer, Tom Harrison, to comply with Brunel's wish for low piston speed, high track speed and light axle loading; the Brunellian concept was, as usual, far ahead of its time but

Harrison's design rose to the occasion with an engine seventy or more years ahead of its time in some ways* though as far as 1838 was concerned its unreliability made it of little use to the Great Western Railway.

It was a train in itself. First came the engine carriage, a flat platform, fenced around to stop the driver falling off or falling into one of the four, 6-ft diameter driving wheels, which were coupled together in the usual way and driven by two cylinders mounted between the frames at the rear end of the assembly, next to the boiler carriage. The latter was a six-wheeled vehicle carrying a very powerful boiler and behind this came the four-wheeled tender with coke and water. The boiler's firebox was a relatively large one and was divided down the centre by a water-filled partition† to improve the circulation of hot water from the furnace and thus improve steam-raising capability. The fireman had, in effect, two fireboxes to feed and sometimes found difficulty in keeping them both alight, the problem becoming acute when lighting the fires in the morning; one side of the box would refuse to burn at all while the other side burnt merrily. Steam was delivered to the cylinders through pipes bridging the gap between the two vehicles, each pipe having a ball and socket joint to allow for the movements of each carriage. The connecting rods drove the crankshaft which turned in bearings in the frames directly above the leading axle of the engine carriage and a cog on the crankshaft engaged with another on the axle below to effect a geared drive that made the 6-ft driving wheels the equivalent of 16 ft diameter. The driver stood in solitary state on the flat, engine carriage in some peril from the spokes of the driving wheels whirling round just outside the railings while the fireman stoked the furnace from the usual position. Seventy-seven miles an hour has been claimed

---

* The idea of separating boiler and engine in order to make each more powerful and to spread the weight was used by Beyer Peacock with great success from 1909 onwards.

† O. V. Bullied used a somewhat similar device in his phenomenally powerful streamlined engines for the Southern Railway in 1941.

for this engine – running without a train – though it should be pointed out that the claimant also said that the driver worked the slide valves by hand – a feat beyond the physical capabilities of any man with 3 tons in steam pressure forcing the valves to their seatings, though the idea of the driver frantically wrenching the supposed hand-levers back and forth in time with the pistons at 77 mph has its humorous side.

The entire broad-gauge system was under attack in 1838 and indeed for years before and after, chiefly over the question of which was the best gauge. Unfortunately the broad gauge had not been first on the scene and Brunel was bitterly attacked by the Liverpool contingent among his own shareholders – the 'Northern Party' – who, deep inside standard gauge territory were painfully aware of the disadvantages of trying to work two gauges in one, small, island, and it was their demand for an Inquiry which led to John Hawkshaw's ill-natured report which in turn led to Brunel offering his resignation. Brunel's most persistent critic was a theoretician – and one who could not do his sums – the first of the Doctors who have, from time to time, plagued the railway: the superbly named Dr Dionysius Lardner. He had been the main witness for the Parliamentary opposition to the Great Western in 1835 when they chose for their target 'that monstrous and extraordinary, most dangerous and impracticable tunnel at Box'. One 'engineer' said that the noise of two trains passing inside the tunnel would be loud enough 'to shake the nerves of this assembly'. On being asked what sort of noise this would be, the man replied, 'I do not know but no one would be induced to go twice.' Dionysius, for his contribution to the learned debate, produced some complicated calculations to 'prove' that if the train's brakes should fail as it entered the tunnel, running down the gradient, it would emerge at the horrifying speed of 120 mph – 'at which no human could breathe'. Brunel pointed out that the Doctor had not taken into account the retarding effect of friction in moving parts nor of atmospheric resistance and the true speed in such circumstances would be nearer 55 mph. Lardner, the conjuror of figures, was exposed but in doing so Brunel handed to the Sage a new stick with which to beat the broad gauge – atmospheric resistance – and from that day forth Lardner used it at every possible opportunity.

Brunel's great, brick bridge over the Thames at Maidenhead was another favourite target for the 'anti' brigade. Here Brunel had to carry his railway across the approximately 200-ft wide river and instead of using a series of conventional arches he made use of a midstream island and cleared the water in two huge, 128-ft leaping spans, springing onto and off the island and if this were not audacious enough he built the arches to have a rise of only 24 ft 6 in. from the 'springing' of the arch to its crown so that, with a 128-ft span, they looked almost flat and not arches at all. Reflected in unruffled water they form ellipses so perfectly proportioned as to appear quite undated even now, 147 years on. Everyone knew they would fall down – the arches were too flat – and when, in May 1838, the timber centering on which the arches had been built was eased away from the bricks, the bricks sagged. 'Gaps you may place your arm into' appeared between the rows; the 'I-told-you-so' brigade had a field day and Brunel's resignation was demanded by the 'Liverpool Party'. To Brunel the fuss was just another 'bearish ploy' by the Stock Exchange though that belief did not make his beleaguered life any easier. In fact there was very little wrong with the bridge. Contractor Chadwick had moved the centerings before the cement had properly set and some bricks on each side of the crown of the eastern arch had sagged half an inch. Chadwick put the job right at his own expense and in October successfully eased the timber supports and would have removed them altogether but Brunel, having suffered much unnecessary harrassment over them, decided they could provide him with an enormous and elaborate joke – he ordered them to be left in place, looking for all the world as if they were supporting the bridge but in fact standing clear of them. Few people knew the arches were free-standing, the 'I-told-you-so' brigade changed their tune to 'Wait-and-see' and Brunel had the best part of a year to enjoy his practical joke – of suitably gigantic, Brunellian, proportions – before a great storm in the autumn of 1839 blew all the useless timber away and left the bridge standing pristine and perfect.

Not all the scientific community was against Brunel. Charles Babbage, the great mathematician of the age, was very much for him. One evening at a dinner held by the British Association when Babbage was President of the Association and George Stephenson was Vice-President, Babbage waited till Stephenson had started his second glass of champagne and was suitably mellowed then asked him, 'Mr Stephenson, if no railways existed yet you were in full possession of all the knowledge of railways you now possess and you were consulted respecting the gauge for the first railway, would you advise the gauge of four feet eight and a half inches?'

'Not exactly that gauge,' replied the Father of Railways. 'I would take a few inches more – but only a few.'

A great deal of spectacular but unglamorous pick-and-shovel work was put in at and below ground-level by the unknown navvies in order that the great, Brunellian concepts could be realised. The site of Paddington station was on ground sloping south on the south side of the Paddington arm of the Grand Junction canal; thousands of cartloads of clay and rubble were shovelled over the area to level it up; foundations had to be dug for bridge piers and large buildings; and sometimes the engineering of earlier centuries got in the way. At Westbourne Green, for example, in the fields below Lord Hill's mansion, the navvies were hacking away with pick and shovel, preparing the ground for the big, polygonal engine house when they struck the arch of an ancient sewer standing solid as a reef of rocks across the path of Great Western progress. There was no choice but to blast the old bricks away, yet to break through the crown of the arch, into the passage, to lay a charge of gunpowder was almost impossible. After a fierce struggle with picks and heavy hammers the navvies made a breach sufficient to lower into the tunnel a fused mine of black powder. Brunel's Chief Assistant,

R. P. Brereton, was in charge with his Foreman, Mr Brown.
They fixed the slow-burning fuse, lit it and retired to a safe
distance. Nothing happened. Brereton waited for double the
length of time the fuse needed to burn through to the charge and
then, with Mr Brown and a Scots labourer, he came out from
behind his cover and walked forward to investigate what they
thought was a dud mine. It exploded. The three men were
thrown yards by the blast, which was heard a mile away, and
were buried under a storm of ancient bricks and mortar. They
were carried unconscious to the Red Lion, their faces a mass of
blood, clothes ripped. Brereton was unconscious for an hour
but he and Brown were able to go home later. The Scot never
went home again – he died the same evening in hospital.

A continuously explosive situation existed among the navvies
as a result of English and Scots antagonism towards Irishmen
employed or hoping to be employed on the works. Religion was
not the issue; if trouble flared it was because the Irish, desperate
for work, were offering to labour for less money – either as an
incentive to the Foreman to take them on and thus displace a
higher paid man or else to remain at work for less money at a
time of lay-offs.

On 27 April 1838 a large body of Irishmen arrived on the
works at Ealing and asked to be taken on, offering to work for
less than those already employed. It was a Sunday but the
Catholic Irish already on the works had not stopped work for
that reason, nor had the other men and when the word passed
round – like wildfire – that some 'Irishers' were offering to come
in for less wages and that therefore an equal number of English,
Scots and Irish were likely to be laid-off, there occurred, in the
words of *The Times*, 'a desperate and alarming affray with
atrocities on both sides, brutal and unmanly' and this continued until the cavalry, in the form of the 12th Lancers,
intervened with the flat – and not always the flat – of their
swords. The navvies at work then went on strike at this armed
intervention in their private arbitration and refused to go back
to work until the army and the would-be navvies had been sent

on their way. The first fight was over but the law required that bodies be arrested for this breach of the peace so the soldiers impartially arrested twenty-four from each side, handed them over to the newly formed and hated 'Peelers' who lodged them all in Clerkenwell gaol where the hungry newcomers may at least have had a meal after all their hard bargaining.

On Monday the men were still 'out' and the other party were still standing by with their offer of cut-price labour. On Tuesday those navvies who had been employed came to the works, formed meetings to discuss the situation and decide what to do whilst past the big, noisy groups of tough navvies, each carrying his sharp spade or pick handle, rode the brightly uniformed cavalry, warily patrolling the line up and down from Ealing to Acton.

On Wednesday morning, early, two Metropolitan policemen based at Brentford, were keeping watch on the railway cutting in Hanger Lane and saw a group of becudgelled navvies moving swiftly across the field towards the railway line with such earnestness of purpose that could mean only one thing – it was an outflanking movement by a group of newcomer navvies who intended to thrash those in possession off the work. Regardless of the odds against them the constables drew their truncheons, climbed the field gate and raced over the grass to take the company in the rear. The surprise was complete and they managed to grab one man but as they were carrying him off, the shouts and yells of the fray attracted the attention of other men who rushed to the scene waving pick-axe handles and shouting enthusiastic threats. The constables, like the great Duke of Wellington, knew when to retreat, very wisely relinquished their prisoner and hurried back to Brentford police station as their man was hoisted shoulder-high by his mates and carried gloriously from the conflict.

At three o'clock that afternoon the entire constabulary muster of Brentford, Ealing and Acton, armed with cutlasses and led by their Inspectors on horseback, marched on the Acton section of the line to arrest the escapee and at least some of those who had helped him escape. Navvy sentries posted along the track bed saw the police coming and roused their mates, sitting around the fires and lying under makeshift shelters, with dramatic cries of 'Warhawk' so that by the time the police had reached the line several hundred navvies, armed with their own special weapons, had massed across the cutting to meet them. The Chief Inspector asked for the men who had been involved in the rescue from police custody to be given up – and was greeted with a roar of derision, cudgels were raised and the men surged one step forward with defiant cheers. The police stood their ground – to have backed away an inch would have precipitated a massacre – and the Chief Inspector damped the navvies' ardour slightly by pointing out that, while they out-numbered his men for the moment, the navvies would have to fight a regiment of cavalry within minutes of any brawl starting with the police 'so would it not be better to give up those men I have named?' After a noisy confrontation the labourers gave way, allowed the police to go in amongst them and arrest three men: John Sawyer, William Marshall and Charles Englefield. Sawyer was fined £5 or two months' gaol for resisting arrest, the others were fined £2 or one month in gaol for obstruction.

And while the campaigning season was in full swing, Brunel's railway was not being built; the opening date to the public of 4 June 1838 to which the Company had committed itself in print began to look uncomfortably close.

Ten miles west of Maidenhead bridge the contract to exca-vate Sonning cutting lay in the impecunious hands of Mr William Ranger, the man who had already failed in his work for Brunel on tunnelling near Bristol. At Sonning a cutting two miles long and up to 60 ft deep – three million cubic yards of clay, a waterlogged nightmare for eight months of the year – had to be removed with nothing more potent than a horse-drawn wheel-barrow up the cutting side. One hundred horses and 750 men were all the forces Ranger could muster and his money was being carried away faster than the Sonning clay. In February the operation was, literally, bogged down in a quagmire of slimy clay and on Saturday 19 May Ranger finally ran out of money, was unable to pay his men for the preceding week's slog and, instead of telling them the truth, he asked them to work another week and to be paid for two weeks then. The navigators, being a reasonable, if somewhat trusting crowd, agreed. But the following Saturday, 26 May, William Ranger was not to be found and the delicate task of breaking the dreadful news to the navvies he left, in the most cowardly fashion, to his pay clerk. Even then, all might have been well – the navvies knew that it was not the clerk's fault if they were not paid and would not have taken their annoyance out of his skin. Unfortunately, the pay clerk, perhaps out of fear, adopted a very high-handed manner and when the first man stepped up to be paid, he snapped, 'There's no money this week,' and slammed the pay window shutter down. It was not the wisest plan. Immediately there was a scrimmage. A pair of navvies split the door of the pay-hut asunder with a few blows of their mighty spades, stormed in, dragged out the tactless clerk and beat him senseless while the others demolished the hut and every other building on the site. Having sealed Ranger's fate as a contractor by smashing every bit of plant in sight they set out en masse for Reading in the hope of finding someone to whom they could complain – they knew Mr Brunel was a fair man; perhaps, they thought, they could get a message to him. Sweeping up the labourers working on the embankments between the unfinished cutting and the town, they entered Reading one thousand strong – but peaceably, being honourable men and having no complaint against the townspeople. They congregated in the Forbury near the centre of the town and soon the Mayor, Mr Billings, came to them with a letter – from whom he did not say – stating that they would be paid two weeks' wages 'next Wednesday'. At this assurance, from the mouth of the Mayor of Reading, the simple workmen relaxed visibly and the inhabitants felt no more alarm at their presence on the site of what had once been a Viking encampment. But the Billings' method was only a stop-gap to pacify the navvies while he sent for the cavalry from Windsor and the following day a squadron of armoured, sabred Horse Guards came cantering into the town with Captain Biddulph and Cornet Fitzgerald at their head.

The navvies, camped peacefully on the Forbury grass, smoking their pipes whilst their wives cooked the food they had bought on credit – on the strength of Billings' letter – were thrown into a state of alarm at the arrival of this clanking panoply of war. Someone, they reasoned, must be expecting trouble and trouble can come only if we are not, after all, going to get paid. The town's shopkeepers, drawing the same conclusion, hastily put the shutters up over the windows. Billings had sown alarm and tension throughout the erstwhile peaceful town but he had control of the situation with overwhelming strength and no one need pay the hungry men.

Many were indeed beginning to starve and in groups they circulated the town, asking for money or food and the inhabitants, with feelings of pity mixed with a strong dash of self-preservation, paid up. The Vikings were back in the Forbury for the first time since Alfred the Great and Danegeld was the order of the day. For a full week the navigators were fed by the town and on Friday 1 June they were asked to congregate in the Forbury to hear what had been decided for them.

The Mayor and Mr Blandy, a solicitor and leading figure in the town, addressed the men, well aware of what might happen if they decided to ignore the cavalry and become angry. Speaking carefully, Mr Billings said he sympathised with their difficulties and complimented them on their good behaviour in the face of privation and mentioned the high regard in which they were held by the townspeople. As to the money they were owed, if the men would leave the town at once and return to work in the cutting three miles away they would receive three days' pay as they left the Forbury, they would be given three days' pay on the morrow and another three days' pay on Monday. He, Mr Billings, had offered £800 of his own money to the Great Western Directors to insure that this would be done. Mr Blandy then spoke. He, too, praised their forbearance and said that he had agreed to loan the Great Western sufficient money from his personal account to cover six days' wages for every man – six to nine days' pay was therefore covered and, he urged, they would be very foolish not to close with this offer as any other action would at once result in the townspeople losing the high regard they at present entertained for the navvies. He tactfully omitted to mention the cavalry but the iron-shod hooves of the Horse Guards scraped impatiently on the cobbles over by the Abbey Gateway to give a weightier reason for accepting the offer. So with little more than promises and these covering at most nine of the fourteen days of arrears, the navvies turned away with a great groan of exasperation and made their way back to the workings. The settlement was a strange business. The men had not met an official of the Great Western Railway or Mr Ranger with whom they might have argued the matter and got their due arrears; instead they were dealt with by two men who had no connection at all with the railway but who, as Mayor and lawyer, possessed the legal means of enforcing any settlement they chose by means of the Riot Act – and the cavalry.

While Sonning cutting lay deserted and its hungry navvies prowled the streets of Reading, the Directors of the Great Western Railway were preparing for their private opening of the line several days in advance of the public opening. Two trains, each capable of carrying 400 people, were marshalled at Paddington, booked to start at 11.15 a.m. and 11.45 a.m. on Thursday 31 May 1838 and to run out twenty-two and a half miles to a temporary terminus situated on the east bank of the Thames and rather optimistically called 'Maidenhead' when 'Taplow' would have been nearer the truth. The first train from Paddington left fifteen minutes late hauled by the Company's only reliable engine, *North Star,* which hauled its train without incident at astonishing speeds approaching 40 mph. The coaches jolted over track which had only recently been ballasted, had never been travelled over at speed so that all the 'hills and hollows' were just lying there, waiting to be discovered. Bearing this in mind, top speeds of 40 mph seem a little reckless but the passengers did not think so and were delighted – 'smoother than the London & Birmingham' they said as they toured the station and engine shed at Maidenhead. After looking round they rejoined their train which transported them to Salt Hill, near Slough, where a Great Western Director and merchant banker, Mr G. H. Gibbs, had provided a banquet in marquees erected in his parkland.

A great many toasts were drunk, a few of the party were drunk by the time they returned to the train, finding some difficulty in mounting the ladders into the coaches but eventually they were all stowed and hoisted safely aboard and *North Star* was unleashed – as if the driver and fireman had drunk a toast or two themselves. Soon the coaches were jostling, bounding along, breaking the Directors' 40 mph speed limit. The rapid, down-up, down-up movement of the carriages together with the triple jarring hammer from three pairs of wheels over the rail joints made many passengers lose interest in the future of the line and to regret the lobster, champagne and claret of the recent past but there were some who thrived on the excitement. Bristol Director T. R. Guppy frothed over like freshly opened 'bubbly' and, opening the door of his compartment, climbed onto the roof of the carriage and proceeded to walk – or totter – from end to end of the train, somehow managing to jump the gaps between the bucking coaches and even retaining sufficient presence of mind to lie down as the train passed through bridges. Whether alarm or anxiety was engendered by this feat of inebriation is not recorded but the train neither stopped nor even slackened speed and arrived at Paddington in only thirty-four minutes from Salt Hill, nineteen miles away, with Mr Guppy still intact on the roof.

THREE

Imprisoning the Passengers

The original scheme for the Great Western's London end was to have joined the London & Birmingham Railway at Willesden and to have shared their Euston terminus. Luckily for us the L&BR put such difficulties in the way of this that the Great Western was forced to build a new line from Acton to Paddington, starting the work in October 1837 – the very month that had been advertised for the opening of their line out of Euston. The revised opening date, 4 June 1838, was kept – just – with the trains leaving a hastily thrown together Paddington station and, in places, running over unballasted track. The station lay immediately south of the Paddington arm of the Grand Junction canal, six miles from the City of London. A few streets lay to the east, around the canal basin, but north beyond the canal, west and south lay virtually rural country: meadows, brooks, market gardens, pleasant parks around the mansions of the rich. The Great Western opened a booking office in Prince's Street, near the Bank of England and for 6d carried passengers in a horse-drawn omnibus to their Paddington terminus, calling to pick up at several inns along Oxford Street before turning north into Edgware Road, around the canal basin and along London Street up to the gates of the railway terminus.

The entrance was divided into IN and OUT passages by a central gatehouse, the iron gates hinged on stone pillars and latched against the house when closed. 'Plain but serviceable', reported the ever-critical *Sun*. Passing through the gate, the omnibus passengers had the goods shed on their left, the canal at a slightly higher level on their right and in front the new, white bricks of the many-arched Bishop's Road bridge which carried that thoroughfare over the station and sheltered beneath its arches the railway's offices. A central arch was open to admit road traffic to the main booking office and platforms, most were bricked in and pierced with windows to light the offices within but at the southern end a low veranda sheltered a 'pedestrians-only' entrance to a second booking hall.

Inside, the station was formed with a single platform, its south face for departing trains, the north face for arrivals. Spindly, cast-iron columns supported the plain, slated roof, the walls were merely planks like a barn – indeed, it looked similar to the Euston terminus the Great Western had been prevented from using. The L&BR was the supreme arbiter of railway good taste at the time so Paddington station received neither praise nor blame – all eyes were on the track and train. Lack of ballast showed the massively timbered, wide-gauge track to its best advantage, the impression of strength enhanced by the vista of complicated point-work from the platform's end. 'Sturdy and businesslike' it was called and those who had already become used to the narrow, coalcart-gauge tracks of the L&BR were particularly impressed. The engines, too, ranged outside their polygonal engine-house a little to the west of the platform, looked stable and powerful, straddling the wide tracks on huge wheels – especially the totally unorthodox *Thunderer* – an engine which was a train as well. Jim Hurst was with *Vulcan* on the morning of the public opening, acting as stand-by pilot while *Aeolus* was at the head of the first train. That Jim Hurst, personal friend of Daniel Gooch and the Great Western's No. 1 driver, had not been given the honour of driving the first train may be set down, in fairness perhaps, to some minor fault in *Vulcan* rather than to any fault in Jim though, even at that early stage, when his opportunity for driving Great Western trains had been on nothing more than ballasting jobs, he had shown something of his old L&MR form and had been involved in a collision or two.

The reporter from the *Sun* (a paper always hostile to Brunel) was feeling particularly hostile that first morning – and not just because he had been ordered out into the wilds of the Parish of St Marylebone at an unearthly hour on a Monday morning; he had not been invited to attend the Directors' 'beano' the previous Thursday but now had to queue with the rest to buy his ticket to sample the delights or otherwise of Great Western trains. He walked up the platform running his prejudiced eyes over the chocolate-brown carriages: Posting carriages, 1st class, closed 2nd class and open-sided 2nd class. There were no 3rd class carriages on the Great Western in 1838. With a candour that did him credit he admitted that they were an enormous improvement on the L&BR. They were, he reported, 12 ft from rail to roof, so tall that a man could stand upright in them. The Posting carriages he called 'Extra-1st class' and compared them to 'the most luxurious saloon on a river steamer'. They had couches on which one could recline and, even more wonderful, 'tables at which you may sit and read or play chess'.

The reporter from the *Berkshire Chronicle*, ordered out from Reading to cover events at Maidenhead station, got out of bed at five o'clock that Monday morning to catch a stage-coach called 'The Railway' which started at 6.30 a.m. on a new shuttle service between the county town and the terminus at Maidenhead. The coach was hauled by two horses and was grossly overladen but Driver Kibble handled his pair with skill, keeping them hard up to the collar yet controlling their effort so that they lasted the stages at a good speed. Horses were changed at Twyford and Knowle Hill and the conveyance drew up in the station yard below the embankment dead on time, having covered the fourteen miles in one hour inclusive of stops. The passengers and sightseers hurried up a long flight of steps and passed through the booking hall to gain the wooden platform where a train of six coaches hauled by the locomotive *Apollo* was waiting to leave. The up and down platforms were sheltered under a pitched roof, the offices, refreshment room and waiting rooms were within the walls on the north side while the south side was open to the elements, the roof eaves being supported on iron columns.

The trains left Paddington and Maidenhead simultaneously at 8 a.m. with little fuss and no ceremonial unless you count the firing of some cannon as the trains passed the half-built Ealing station. *Aeolus* arrived at Maidenhead in ninety minutes from Paddington and was cheered on arrival by some workmen and a few townspeople. The journey had been a suspiciously long one and rumour since has had it that she burst a boiler tube on the way down and had to be pushed through by the following train – but whatever the cause, she was not late because the Company had taken the wise precaution of not issuing any arrival times.

Passengers could join or leave the trains at West Drayton station and at Slough – where there was no station. This was because the Provost of Eton had, apparently, a very low opinion of his scholars and had forbidden any station or platform to be built within three miles of the College on the grounds that the proximity of a train to whisk his boys to London would be 'injurious to their morals' and furthermore he ordered that a boy-proof fence be erected on each side of the railway in the vicinity of Slough and that 'a good and sufficient number of men' be employed to prevent the boys from getting on the line. The Provost obviously suspected that his boys would decamp to the fleshpots of London at the first opportunity and forced these conditions and prohibitions into the 1835 Act of Parliament which Incorporated the Great Western Railway.

These strictures were nothing less than the Law of the Land and the Company was forced into complicated manoeuvres to circumvent them. They diverted a length of highway which led to the line, built a new road for the public and turned the old road into a securely fenced path to a public house which they had built near the lineside. This pub, called New House, they leased to a publican and rented back from him two rooms as office and waiting room. While these arrangements were being made the GWR made use of an existing pub called the

Crown, further west along the track; passengers bought their tickets and scrambled up into the carriages from the plain track. The Provost of Eton was furious and took the case to the Lord Chancellor who, being a fair man, ruled that the Great Western Railway could exercise its statutory powers in any way at all provided it did not infringe the strict letter of the law – and public houses were not railway stations.

On 5 June the 5 p.m. up from Maidenhead was hauled by *Aeolus*. The engine ran well and arrived at Slough in good time only to be greeted by a riot of 'an enormous number' of Eton scholars all determined to have their morals corrupted as quickly as possible. Ignoring the necessity of buying a ticket they had fought their way past porters, regular policemen and the extra men employed to keep them off the line – the fight being a continuous one as they struggled to remain by the line until the train arrived. As soon as it stopped it was stormed by the scholars and for a full twenty-five minutes another brawl ensued as the boys climbed onto the roofs of their rightful conveyances – the 1st class carriages – or scrambled in over the sides of the open 2nds and slummed it to the great alarm of the 2nd class occupants. Eton, outnumbering the Great Western, won and the train left twenty-five minutes late packed to the roof-tops with upper-class hooligans – the judges, bishops, generals and politicians of the future. If only the *Sun* had published some names!

Maidenhead station yard in 1838–9 was thronged with road coaches awaiting passengers or waiting to be pulled up into the sidings for loading onto rail. Teams of horses, as aristocratic as their owners, polished, harness immaculate, stood tethered, liveried servants in high boots and cockaded hats tending them. Stage-coach drivers and guards haunted the refreshment rooms up in the station, drinking a tuppenny gin or brandy as they waited for the train to bring their coach down from London. The guard of Cooper's coach was disdainful of the crude railroad – no breeding, no skill – iron horses! Bah! He and his mate were Kings of the Road and he did not mind letting the station staff know it. He strolled arrogantly out of the bar-room, the brandy inside him heating his jealousy, making his heavy boots thud on the miserable, wooden platform as he pulled on his black cheroot. Now, the most heinous crime on the Great Western, after travelling without a ticket, was to smoke anywhere on the Company's property and the guard of Cooper's coach knew it. What did he care? Three times the porter asked him to put out his cheroot. Not he. 'Oh joy!' thought the porter. 'He's been asking for this for days.' Down to the town lock-up, accompanied by the porter and a railway policeman, went the guard of Cooper's coach who saved himself from a court appearance and a fine only by writing from his cell to the GWR Directors a humble plea for mercy.

Mr Bigg was a Great Western train conductor, a superior servant placed in charge of the entire train even, theoretically, the driver. His son rode with him to wait on the 1st class passengers and to keep their carriages clean. He was on the platform at Maidenhead one morning, supervising the stowing and locking-in of each passenger, when a gentleman escorting two ladies came to board the train. His name was Bagley – and he was smoking. Mr Bigg asked him to put out his cigar; Bagley refused; Bigg refused to let him onto the train – for which he had bought a ticket; and Bagley, who was a barrister of King's Bench, exploded, storming away at the upstart valet-cum-conductor with some very colourful language. Mr Bigg thereupon exercised his authority, calling upon a pair of railway policemen who, drawn thither by the sounds of discord, were standing on the edge of the gaping crowd. Between them they marched the barrister, by then speechless with rage, off to the gaol while his ladies sobbingly brought up the rear. Bagley was rather too hot to hold and was very soon released. He wrote to the Great Western Directors demanding that they see him and apologise for their unspeakably dictatorial, damnably un-English servant and, furthermore, to dismiss him in his, Bagley's, presence. The interview was arranged but Mr Bigg was summoned before the Board the day before to give the

Company's side of the story. He had, he said, only carried out the Directors' by-laws and had been subjected to appalling abuse, additionally humiliating for the presence of the ladies. The Directors sent him away with the gentle suggestion that gaoling was over-enthusiastic – especially when a gentleman of obvious wealth was involved – when simple removal from the premises would have answered the Company's purpose just as well.

Mr Bagley turned up at Paddington next day overflowing with confidence and feelings of pure revenge. In his mind's-eye he saw Bigg arrested, tried and executed after a crushing prosecution speech which he had been rehearsing – an exercise that had given him enormous pleasure. These delightful visions and feelings lasted until he confronted the Great Western Board when he was astonished to discover that, far from being apologetic, the Directors were aggressive and told him directly that Great Western by-laws had the force of law that he as a barrister ought to know, that 'No Smoking' was a Great Western by-law and that Mr Bigg – Bagley heard the upstart referred to as 'Mister' in a state of shocked incredulity – was perfectly entitled to have him arrested and not least for using foul language in a public place, in front of ladies, in a manner quite unbecoming to a gentleman. Bagley withdrew in utter confusion and the Directors, feeling that they had been lucky in that they had his bad language to throw back at him, issued a stern warning to all staff not to exercise their powers of arrest except in extreme cases and 'certainly not in pursuance of some private quarrel'.

The trains ran with only a little more supervision than the stage-coaches on the Bath road. On the open track a policeman patrolled a beat two or even three miles long, inspecting the rails for defects, signalling trains, keeping gates shut and preventing trespass. At stations two or more policemen operated points, supervised the passengers and generally enforced the Company's by-laws. They were properly sworn constables with as much power on Great Western property as the newly formed Metropolitan police – the Peelers – had elsewhere and their uniform was modelled on that worn by Sir Robert Peel's men. A Great Western policeman wore a tall, leather-crowned top hat, a tail-coat of 'rifle green' with brass buttons from neck to waist where the coat was cut away square to fall into the long tails and to show the dark trousers. On duty each man wore a black and white wrist-band on his sleeve and carried an 18-in. truncheon painted black with the letters GWR in gold under a gold crown, all shaded in white, green and red. They were supervised by sub-Inspectors and Inspectors under the Chief Inspector, Mr Collard, at Paddington. Inspectors had a broad, red, stripe up each trouser leg and carried their Warrant, written on parchment, rolled inside an ebony tube or baton which was surmounted most auspiciously by a gilt crown. The police looked imposing but as safety devices they were, like the brakes of the time, 'tolerably useless', to quote Brunel. Drivers of passenger trains needed at least a mile in which to stop so, theoretically, they needed a signal visible from at least a mile away. What a driver got was a 6-ft tall policeman standing at the side of the line with his arms raised above his head indicating 'Danger: Stop'. Rear-end collisions were routine.

The Great Western had the means, from May 1838, to signal trains in relative safety with Cooke & Wheatstone's electric telegraph, a clumsy but nonetheless workable system where, in a row of five electro-magnetically induced needles, any two could be deflected to point along converging lines on a dial to indicate a letter. Most of the alphabet was included on the dial so words could slowly be spelt out. The Great Western was the first railway to have the system and installed it by very slow stages at £300 per mile. Questioned about it in Parliament, Charles Saunders, the Company Secretary, was vague as to its applications – guards of trains might be issued with portable instruments which could be plugged into the circuit to give warning of a breakdown or ask for assistance, office work might be speeded up by telegraphing requests instead of sending letters. Possibly because few guards could write nothing was done, perhaps because of cost the ideas were never developed. Certainly, the idea that trains could be signalled in and out of defined sections of track occurred to no one; the device became little more than an expensive toy and the instrument room at Paddington became one of the 'sights' to be visited by the aristocracy, British and foreign.

Brunel and Seymour Clarke, the Traffic Superintendent, were waiting for their train on Hanwell station one morning in April 1839 and, in Clarke's own words, 'playing on the telegraph', when the guard of an up train which had broken down between Hanwell and Paddington brought word back – the train's engine, *Atlas*, had melted her fire-bars and was stationary at Bourne farm. Clarke was able to telegraph Paddington for a fresh engine to rescue *Atlas* and its train and also to warn the police at Paddington so that they could caution the drivers of down trains to take care in the vicinity of the failure in case men were walking about on the line. This was indeed a wonderful example of the vital necessity of the telegraph to any railway; Seymour Clarke was greatly impressed and wrote directly to Charles Saunders so that he might inform the Directors: 'The telegraph was of use today . . .' The wires got to West Drayton in July 1840 but soon after the system broke down and was not repaired for three years.

The police and indeed all railway staff were usually close to a pub or refreshment room selling beer and spirits; they usually had a 'bob or two' in their pockets with the inevitable result that men were often drunk on duty. It was hard to discourage, it was a continuation of the coaching tradition and in any case something of a national pastime and the Company took a lenient view, especially in those very early days when the rakish Regency habits were still fresh in everyone's memory. When the conductor of a train from Maidenhead was accused of drunkenness by the passengers, the Maidenhead station master wrote in mitigation to the Directors: 'He had drunk no more than usual and his vital powers were not affected.' He was let off with a fine.

Policemen operating points (or switches as they were called in 1838–45) were called switchmen and were paid a shilling a week more than the 'common constables' patrolling the line. Some of the original police/switchmen at Maidenhead were Bill Hubbard, Jim Spreadbury, Tom Reeves and Henry Barefoot who brought his young son onto the railway as a messenger boy and, Barefoot junior, keeping out of serious trouble, became in his time a policeman and later a signalman, completing sixty-two years' service with the GWR. The switchman walked the layout operating the points by hand-levers, remembering if possible, how each point lay. After a spell of shunting, Tom Reeves and Jim Spreadbury, feeling thirsty, hurried away for a jar or two before the next down train arrived. Unfortunately they had forgotten the points in the down main line, just before the platform, which they had set for the carriage shed when the last shunt placed some coaches there. Michael John Almond, driving *Lion* on the next down train, had his speed well under control on the approach to Maidenhead and, alert as ever, noticed the points set wrong but, brakes being what they were, was quite unable to stop in time so the train swerved into the siding and trundled through the shed driving the carriages through the end wall and onto *Olde England* which finally brought the impetuous *Lion* to a stand.

Reeves and Spreadbury heard the dreadful, if somewhat distant, noise and hurried back to the track where they were at once pounced upon by their sub-Inspector, Mr O'Rourke. Being somewhat tipsy they unwisely gave frivolous answers to his questions and O'Rourke reported them to Inspector Duffy for drunkenness. Just for that they might well have got off with a fine but Duffy, for reasons of his own or simply out of zeal, added legalistically the corollary charges of 'absence without leave' and 'laziness'. Reeves and Spreadbury, up before the Directors, got the sack. Chief Inspector Collard was displeased at the dismissals though why he should have concerned himself with two backsliding constables is not clear. At any rate, a few days after they were sacked he went down to Maidenhead and booked Inspector Duffy for being drunk on duty. Collard brought Duffy before the Board and gave the Directors his eyewitness account of the Inspector's insobriety. The Chief had spoken and it looked bad for Duffy. Asked what he had to say, Duffy stoutly declared his innocence and produced a letter from a clergyman, a letter testifying to his good, sober character, a letter so powerful that the Directors were no longer able to believe their own Chief Policeman – an eyewitness to the crime – and let Duffy off without so much as a token fine. There the matter rested until Duffy's assistant, O'Rourke, weeks after his boss had been exonerated, decided to strike a blow in his defence, a blow against the Collard camp, by going up to Paddington and arresting for drunkenness Inspector Jack Higgins. Higgins duly went before the Board and produced in his defence a testimonial from his ex-Colonel. Unfortunately for Higgins, Colonels carried no weight with Great Western Directors and Higgins was sacked. Back down to Maidenhead came Collard, looking for revenge, caught O'Rourke drunk and hauled him before the Board. O'Rourke was obviously not one of the brightest policemen on the Great Western – in spite of what had happened to his victim Higgins, the Irishman could do no better than a Colonel's testimonial and was promptly sacked. With honours even the feud died and appeared no more in the Company's records.

Out along the line between Slough and West Drayton, a common constable with the splendidly apt name of Broomhead, patrolled a lonely beat and slipped off for a quick and often not so quick pint whenever he thought he had an opportunity. He was away from the line one morning when a farmer came to a gate with his cows for his regular crossing to the pasture. Broomhead had forgotten him; so the farmer helped himself by opening the gates to let the cows over the line but then rather dropped the policeman into the mire by failing to close them behind him. They swung out on their hinges, foul of the line, and the very next train crashed into them doing the engine no damage but shattering the gates to firewood. Poor Broomhead devised a good rigmarole by the time he was taken before the Board, explaining how he had insufficient warning of the approach of a train (the line was virtually straight for miles in each direction) and so he often found it difficult, even dangerous, to get the gates closed in time. It was a bold effort and they therefore docked only 5 of his 17 shillings that week. One morning, a few weeks later, quite unworried by his previous narrow escape, Broomhead went to the pub, came back in time to wave an up and a down train past and then, with 'nothing about for an hour', sank into the grass for a refreshing nap. Unfortunately for him the contractors were making use of the empty time to run some ballast out on the up line between West Drayton and Slough. Doubly unfortunate for him was that the engine was Gooch's pride and the Company's only hope, *North Star*, driven by Harry Appleby. It was working in the 'wrong' direction – that is, travelling down the up line – with the engine nearest Slough.

The 'ballast' gradually worked closer to the slumbering Broomhead, time passed and no one was making a 'Danger' signal to protect the working train. The next up passenger train left Slough more or less on time, hauled by *Lion*, driven by the Great Western's best driver, Michael Almond from Tyneside. The line ahead was virtually straight. Almond was keeping a sharp look-out as usual, saw the tall chimney of *North Star* – and braked with every means at his disposal, which was not much. Workmen leapt off wagons, Appleby and his fireman abandoned their engine, jumping right and left as *Lion*, whistle blowing, driving wheels turning backwards and its tender's wooden brake blocks smouldering, rapidly closed the gap and finally crashed into Gooch's pride and joy. The sound of whistles and rending metal finally woke Broomhead, who rose bleary-eyed and grassy from the lineside, trying to take in the scene before him – two trains head-on when only seconds before, it seemed to him, the line was to have been empty for an hour.

The two Geordies, Almond and Appleby, stormed in to give him their estimation of his worth in furiously unintelligible dialect while the contractor's men stood around with broad grins, enjoying the show.

'You've only lost a buffer off *Star* – and bent her beam a bit,' protested Broomhead when the other two stopped to draw breath.

'Is that all?' snapped Almond. 'Wait till Mr *Gouch* sees it – he'll have your job.'

No one hurt *North Star* and got away with it. Not only did the negligent Broomhead lose his job and the innocent Almond – a Gooch 'original' from Robert Stephenson's works – was fined the sum of £5 which he paid off in £1 weekly instalments but his doubly innocent fireman, John Horner, was fined £2 10s at 5 shillings a week.

What one crashed into made a great deal of difference to one's fate. Three weeks and three pounds after the Broomhead incident, Michael Almond on *Lion* was approaching Paddington with an up passenger train. The police, under Inspector Dixon, were shunting with *Vulcan,* driven by Jim Hurst, and had placed four carriages on the up main line, west of Westbourne bridge some 500 yds from the station. As usual Dixon had not sent a man back to protect the stationary carriages; they had gone on with their engrossing work and forgotten about the up train. Without a distant warning Michael was going far too fast to avoid the abandoned carriages and hit them so hard that the carriage furthest from the impact cannoned away, breaking its coupling with the rest, jumped the tracks and shivered into matchwood against the pillar of Westbourne bridge. Knowing he still had two weeks' fine to pay for the last pile-up – for which he was blameless – Michael got down from the dented *Lion* and gave Dixon a large piece of his tormented mind. However, he need not have worried: he had damaged only a carriage, Gooch was not interested in carriages, nor yet in such locomotive freaks as *Lion*. Michael was let off with a caution and Dixon survived to grow old in the Company's service at Reading.

An acute shortage of siding space at all stations and

particularly at Paddington forced the police to use the main line as a temporary dump when they were delving into a siding to extract a wagon from its nether end – all would have been well on these occasions if a man had been sent back a mile beyond the vehicles left on the main line to give a 'Danger' signal to approaching trains but this would have cost the shunting team a man and wasted time in walking – so they tried to do it 'in between' the trains. A coke wagon from the engine shed at Paddington had been left on the up main line just short of the arrival platform and stood there forgotten until the police heard an up train approaching, looked and to their dismay saw that it was hauled by *North Star*. Half a dozen men, policemen and labourers, rushed to put their shoulders to the wagon and together they heaved it clear of the main line and onto the engine siding. Sadly, in their frantic haste each thought the other had altered the points from siding to main line so that when they reversed the truck to roll it along the siding to the fuel stage it instead rolled back out onto the main line, coinciding perfectly with the incoming locomotive and neatly taking off its near-side buffer. Alas! The engine was *North Star*. One man of the gang was chosen to be the guilty one and the rest had a whip-round to provide a 'fiver' to pay for his fine.

FOUR

Driver's Nightmare

The first drivers to work on the Great Western Railway were Lancastrians, Geordies or Scots working on Tyneside, known to Daniel Gooch personally from his early working days and hand-picked by him. For 44 shillings a week they worked any hours required, in any weather, unprotected by cab or signalling from the worst that the weather or fate could throw at them. Some were surly, some notoriously mean, others were very cheerful but all were tough men, intensely proud of themselves and jealous of their craft. They wore a uniform of white corduroy cap, jacket and trousers which the Company rules required – and which they themselves supplied. The rules also required that their clothes should be white and clean each Monday morning but such was their personal pride that they would probably have done this anyhow. Their engines were always burnished as far as the design would allow and an eyewitness has written that the combination of polished locomotives and white-clothed enginemen made 'a stirring sight'. Brunel was well aware of the morale-raising effect of 'spit and polish' and wrote to Tom Harrison of R. W. Hawthorn Ltd, urging him to take more care in embellishing the products of his works: 'We have a splendid engine of Stephenson's [*North Star*] which would be an ornament in the most elegant drawing room and we have another of Quaker-like simplicity taken to the point of shabbiness but very possibly as good an engine but the difference in the care bestowed by the enginemen, the favour in which the elegant one is held by the men, the public and oneself is striking. A plain young lady, however amiable, is apt to be neglected.'

The warmth and humanity of Brunel's kind nature shows up clearly in those few lines and especially in the last sentence. However, the Great Western needed more than polished brass to change its tarnished image. Of the twenty-three engines supplied to the Company during 1838–40, only the four 'Stars' – Gooch designed and Stephenson built – were at all reliable and of those four *North Star* seemed to be dogged with the worst possible luck and was frequently in works for long periods as a result of collision damage. Gooch lived literally in the engine-houses, sleeping in a carriage, trying to work day and night with his fitters to keep his lame-duck fleet on the rails, carrying out running repairs on some while totally rebuilding others, hoping always to have enough engines for the next day's service. In taking down *Vulcan* for rebuilding he discovered that the cylinders were badly out of line with the crankshaft while the blast pipe – which took exhaust steam from the cylinders and discharged it up the chimney – was badly positioned, did not direct the blast centrally and therefore did not draw the fire up as brightly as it ought.

In 1838 the crew of fitters at Paddington shed were all Geordies, craftsmen who operated their own form of 'closed shop' – they recognised no man as a craftsman who had not been trained in Tyneside or at least in the north of England and would not work with any southerner. Gooch was desperately short of skilled men and recruited a Londoner, Mr Gregory, who had been in charge of the engines of a Thames steamboat but had never been north of Watford; he was introduced into the Paddington works and the Geordie fitters promptly downed tools. Gooch quickly solved the situation by sending him down to Maidenhead to replace the resident Tynesider who went joyfully to Paddington to join his fellow exiles. Gregory was so successful as a fitter that Gooch – with small logic – promoted him to Shed Foreman, giving him authority over the drivers as well as locomotive repairs. Young Dan may only have wanted to reward Gregory's hard work but he had made an error of judgement for which Gregory paid dear. The new Shed Foreman was neither an engine driver nor foreman material; the drivers at once resented an outsider being placed over them and started to misbehave. They came to work late, were slow in getting their engines ready for the road; trains not only started late, some never started at all. Gregory was quite unable to keep order and the shed fell into anarchy.

It was not long before he was up in front of the Board charged with failing to carry out his duties as Shed Foreman. Gooch testified on his behalf, or perhaps he was the prosecution witness, for his evidence was ambiguous, stating that 'while he [Gregory] was in every way an excellent workman he had failed as a foreman'. Poor Mr Gregory, he had not asked for the job in the first place. The Directors decided his fate in their usual, unpredictable way, passing the sentence thus: 'You are undoubtedly a skilled servant and we are very sorry to lose you but we have no option but to dismiss you at once.' They sent him home directly with one month's wages in lieu of notice.

The Storeman at Maidenhead shed was Mr Chettle, who had once been Seymour Clarke's assistant until 'excessive drinking' had led to his demotion. Now, the drivers were paid a bonus for economy in the use of lubricating oil and coke so Mr Chettle, issuing oil if not coke as well, was an important man in the drivers' scheme of things and they made it their policy to 'treat' him whenever they could so that he would do all he could to show their engines' oil consumption on the low side of average.

Driver John Chicken was a particular friend of Chettle's – they drank together for company as well as insurance and anything less 'chicken' than John Chicken could not be imagined; he liked his tot and cared little for the Directors or the public. One breezy day in March 1839 John had prepared his engine for the road at Maidenhead and then, with Mr Chettle, went to the station's refreshment room to prepare himself for the icy blast to come on his cabless locomotive. The two friends drank brandy till departure time and then walked together along the platform as well oiled as the engine. Mr Ayres, a

passenger, noticed John Chicken's unsteady gait and the subsequent rough ride was so thoroughly alarming that he decided
that Chicken must be drunk and reported him accordingly. Up
before the Board Chicken did the usual thing and produced a
testimonial letter protesting his sobriety although the best he
could manage was a letter from Storeman Chettle which stated
– with a remarkable lack of subterfuge: 'I was drinking with
Driver Chicken in the refreshment room at Maidenhead station.
He drank no more than usual and his presence of mind was not
impaired.' Chettle's painfully honest letter – obvious devotion
to his friend – placing himself in jeopardy to give an eyewitness
account of the incident must have impressed the Directors for
they let Chicken off without so much as a caution for drinking
and driving but the devoted Chettle they reprimanded for
drinking on duty.

The drivers were bold men and the Directors, out of their
depth in uncharted waters, were unpredictable in their response
to misdeed. In May 1842 an up train left Slough on a non-stop
run to Paddington and was soon rattling along at 35 mph. At
that stage the driver handed over the footplate to his fireman
and retired, via the carriage roofs, to the rear coach in which sat
the conductor, the guard at his handbrake and a score of
passengers. His journey along the tops of the carriages had
provoked shouts of alarm and anger – though at that stage
passengers were unaware that it was their *driver* who was
walking by; his entry into the rear coach, feet first through the
open side had an effect on the travellers similar to that produced
on chickens when a fox enters the run – panic. He waved them
quiet, assured them that there was absolutely no danger because
the fireman was on the engine and to the utter amazement of the
crowd sat down with the other railwaymen and started to drink
beer from a gallon jar produced from under the seat by the
conductor. They sat and swigged away, passing the jar between
the three of them, until the driver judged it time to go up front to
bring the train under control to stop at Paddington. When the
train stopped and the doors were unlocked, the unleashed flood

of outraged humanity surged into Seymour Clarke's office demanding the instant dismissal of all three men for disgraceful neglect of safety.

The curious outcome of this event was that the conductor who was supposed to be in charge of the train and who had produced the beer was fined 10 shillings, the driver who had left his post was fined £1, and the guard, who had in fact remained at his post whilst supping ale, was dismissed.

If one of the Directors had been on that train the outcome for the men would have been rather different. Driver John Leonard was working the 'short' train from Slough to Paddington which – as a matter of routine – ran up the down line from Slough to West Drayton. At Slough Leonard had invited four friends to share the thrill of a footplate ride made doubly exciting by the danger of 'wrong-road running' – protected from head-on collision only so long as the policeman at West Drayton remembered that the 'short' train was coming up the down line and had not yet arrived. The train arrived at Drayton safely, crossed to the up line and came to a stand by the water hydrant at the east end of the platform. A Director standing on the platform saw the crowded state of the footplate and ordered the train's conductor to clear it of trespassers. John Leonard cared not a fig for conductors and refused to put his mates off. The Director himself ordered Leonard to put them off but the driver cared not a penny piece for Directors and refused while the joy-riders joined in the fun by loudly informing the Director that they had bought tickets and would ride where they liked. They were removed under a strong police escort. The Director settled himself in the train, the conductor gave 'Right Away'. But John Leonard was not 'right' – he was in a deep and furious sulk and fully intended to show the interfering Director and everyone else who was in charge of the train. The argument had taken up the time normally spent in filling the engine's tender so this he now did – very slowly. Twenty minutes later he started off and with great ingenuity contrived to make the twenty-five minute journey stretch out a full two hours. This was no mere prank like leaving the train driverless and drinking beer with the guard. Leonard had defied, in effect, the entire Great Western Board of Directors and Something had to be Done. They took him before Buckinghamshire magistrates charged with 'wilfully making a misconduct in deliberately retarding a train' and was fined £2 with costs. Driver Leonard was not overwhelmed by the sentence but paid the whole sum, there and then, on the nail.

In 1838 there were twenty-four Directors, slightly more than one per mile, outnumbering the drivers almost two to one and making supervision concentrated – something the gallant drivers had to live with along with the defects in their engines. And after all, what were a few businessmen compared to the risks faced daily by the footplatemen? Minor hazards included being derailed by a thoughtless policeman or being involved in a collision resulting from lack of brakes, or a piston taking leave of its connecting rod to depart – through the cast-iron cylinder head – for the surrounding fields to more dangerous events such as cranked axles breaking, boiler tubes bursting to send scalding steam and fire out through the firehole or driving wheels, made of cast iron, shattering like shrapnel.

Just to drive one of the nineteen 'lame ducks' was a nightmare. The worst were the Mather Dixon engines, well known throughout the north for poor workmanship yet the Great Western Directors had bought four, two at the outset and two more after *Premier* and *Ariel* had proved their uselessness. These four would not have run at all but for the extreme ingenuity of the men. *North Star*, with a well-designed boiler, was driven with 4 in. of water covering the firebox crown but the boilers on the Mather Dixon engines were so small (partly due to Brunel's specification) that the steam-collecting pipe was too close to the surface of the boiling water and, if the boiler was filled with a safe amount of water, the incompressible stuff would be carried with the steam into the cylinders where the moving pistons would try to compress it and as a result would burst the cylinder casting or bend a flimsy, Mather Dixon connecting rod.

To distance the water level from the steam pipe and so prevent this 'priming' the fireman kept the water level within the boiler low – ½ in. over the firebox crown. This was fine while the engine was running with the throttle open but when the driver closed the throttle – or regulator – the water level fell, by the law of physics, and promptly uncovered the firebox which unerringly resulted in its being burnt by the white-hot coke.

The solution was simple: the driver did not shut off steam. To stop at a station he put the engine into reverse until speed was sufficiently reduced to complete the stop on the tender hand-brake and that of the guard. The driver then opened the cylinder cocks with the regulator open so that steam continued to flow but did not work on the pistons and the water level in the boiler was maintained. Braking by reversing the engine was common practice on the Great Western for the best part of thirty years for although Brunel had designed his railway specifically for high-speed running he never turned his inventive brain to the problem of how to retard 100 tons of metal running at 40 mph and more; indeed, he was quite blasé about the lack of brakes on his trains, for when a Parliamentary Select Committee asked him how efficient were the brakes on the Great Western he replied with typically Brunellian bantering humour: 'Our brakes are tolerably useless.'

Besides this lack of brakes and the appalling difficulties with boiler water level to which all engines – except the 'Stars' – were more or less subject, the driver of any engine had the constant problem of getting water into his boiler in the first place. In 1838/40 there was no such thing as a steam-operated water injector, nor was there for a generation. Water was forced in against steam pressure by axle- or crosshead-driven pumps so that boiler water level could be raised only while the engine was in motion; hand pumps were tried but the enginemen did not care for pumping against 50 lb psi when there were mechanical means at hand; steam 'donkey pumps' were also fitted to some engines – later – but the Company did not care for the expense. To fill his boiler when 'on the shed' a driver would stand his engine against some solid object, a brick wall or buffer stops, oil the rails and leave the engine to run slowly on the spot which charged the boiler with water but was hard on the driver's oil economy drive. He could drive up and down a siding but without decent brakes this could lead to collisions with other engines on the same errand so the simplest and quickest way was to take the engine for a spin along the main line. But a driver going up line from West Drayton shed would return on the same track – down the up line and many, many times collided or nearly collided with an oncoming passenger train. The driver would be fined 10 shillings or £1 according to the Directors' mood for 'careless pumping on the main line' but so long as siding space was limited in the sheds the practice continued – it was that or burn your boiler which would cost a 'fiver' at least and probably dismissal. Gooch had asked for 'pumping sidings' to be laid in 1840 and when the Directors had saved up enough from drivers' 'careless pumping' fines the first of these was laid in, at Paddington.

The Mather Dixon and Tayleur engines, running with perilously low water, were a driver's nightmare because, in addition to running within ½ in. of burning the boiler continuously, it was that or risk a burst cylinder – when they stopped at stations with their cocks open the boiler water level dropped anyhow as water was turned to steam and was blown away through the open cylinders; if delayed for more than a very few minutes a driver would be forced to uncouple from his train and drive out along the line to refill his boiler. In January 1839 Jim Hurst was driving *Vulcan* – which, by the way, had a broken and patched driving wheel – on an up passenger train when his tender jumped the rails but continued happily enough with its wheels running on the longitudinal sleepers under the metals. Jim let it run until they were close to Paddington and then brought the train to a stand before the diverging tracks ahead could drag the tender and the train sideways and cause damage. Still perfectly calm and thoughtful, Jim uncoupled *Vulcan* from its derailed tender and drove into the terminus to raise the alarm and then drove on shed with *Vulcan* so he could drop its fire before the boiler ran out of water. It was all very engineman-like. Had he stayed with his train the engine's boiler would have been burned when the water level dropped. But the Directors were not railwaymen and took the opposite view. Jim was fined £1 for 'deserting his train and not remaining to assist in re-railing his tender'.

January 1839 was the first great crisis for the Great Western Directors, Brunel and Gooch. Even before the opening of the line many shareholders had shown their antagonism to Brunel and his methods and now, the malcontents were saying, their money had been spent in vast quantities to build Brunel's road, they had been promised a perfectly smooth, high-speed ride behind powerful locomotives and yet the opposite was the case. The proprietors were mad and getting madder. At Brunel's suggestion the Directors asked the famous engineers John Hawkshaw and Nicholas Wood to inspect the line and make recommendations. Hawkshaw suggested pulling the whole thing up and starting again with the coal-cart gauge but Wood tried to go deeper and whilst investigating the faulty track employed Dr Lardner, the Scourge of the Broad Gauge, to experiment with the locomotives, using the best – *North Star*. To his great joy Lardner discovered that to increase *North Star*'s speed he had to reduce her load yet at the same time the fuel consumption 'went through the roof', a sequence of facts he eagerly blamed on the 'atmospheric resistance' of the wide front of the engine and carriage ends. Nicholas Wood included this gem of wishful thinking in his report which also condemned Brunel's technique of fixing the longitudinal sleepers down to piles – the piles, far from holding the track down firmly, were propping it up in the air because the longitudinals sagged into the earth between each set so that the passengers experienced a real switchback-type ride. To travel at 40 mph over such a track would have been an interesting experience.

The report was handed to the Board in early December 1838 and the Bristol contingent – half the Board – promptly lost their remaining confidence in Brunel, to the disgust of the London members. Bristol wanted the gauge narrowed and Brunel to become a co-engineer with Joseph Locke. On 14 December a deputation from both sides of the Board went to Brunel with their proposals for and against him and his broad gauge. Brunel cleverly took the wind out of their sails by telling them that he had already decided that his piling technique was counter-productive and would be abandoned but he said he was 'perfectly convinced that a great fallacy pervades the report where *North Star* is concerned as may be shown by experiment'. He finished by saying that if they wished he would resign in favour of Locke – for a co-engineer he would never be.

After much argument the London view prevailed – Brunel remained in sole charge and he was to start at once to discover what was wrong with *North Star*. In this matter Brunel had the assistance of the inventor of the calculating machine and probably the greatest mathematician of the age, Charles Babbage. Brunel, Gooch and Babbage turned the full focus of their minds to the problem and soon realised that the blast pipe was too narrow, overly restricting the flow of exhaust steam into the engine's chimney and, to compound this evil, they found that the pipe was not discharging dead-centre into the chimney. Throughout Christmas 1838 Brunel and Gooch worked to design and supervise the casting of a new blast pipe which they then fitted with great accuracy and on 29 December, with the full Board of the Great Western in a train as heavy as the heaviest employed by Lardner, *North Star* all but flew from Paddington to Slough and in so doing used but a fraction of the former test's fuel. Brunel made sure the Directors knew why the engine had run so well but otherwise the results were kept secret – to quote Daniel Gooch: 'We kept our trials in this matter very quiet, intending to spring it as a mine against our opponents.'

The shareholders held a meeting at the London Tavern, Bishopsgate, on 9 January 1839 with the anti-Brunel faction well to the fore and the dreaded Dr Lardner there to address them. Brunel, Gooch, Babbage and the London Committee were also there as Lardner took the stage: 'The effects of wind resistance [on the front of broad-gauge engines] are, I believe, underestimated. They have more effect than friction in retarding a train and the results I obtained from recent tests carried out on *North Star* were such that at first I could not believe my own figures.' The crowd sighed and groaned, murmured angrily while Brunel and his friends smiled grimly at each other and bided their time. When Dr Lardner had finished Brunel got up, gave the results of his tests on the engine and, most important, gave the simple, mechanical reasons why the engine had run poorly for Lardner and so well subsequently. Charles Babbage then stood up and gave a speech in support of the broad gauge. Lardner was demolished and the shareholders – for better or worse – voted to follow Brunel and the pure, broad-gauge ideal.

Not that the practical problems of the railway were over – far from it. The supply of locomotive water at Paddington was dispensed from a tank which might have been large enough for the eleven engines and the small service the Company was running in June 1838 but it was certainly too small to supply engine needs by the end of that year with seventeen engines and a more frequent service; Seymour Clarke had asked for a second tank but the request had been ignored. The problem was made far worse because the water was released to the tank from the nearby canal and, naturally enough, the canal company were not terribly concerned with maintaining a good flow or any flow at all. The miserly amount that flowed over their sluice to the engine shed tank was not enough to keep pace with demand during the day so that by evening when the last engine came on shed the tank was nearly empty and the next day's service out of Paddington depended on the tank re-filling overnight. Sometimes the overnight flow would be interrupted for hours so that the 8 a.m. train's engine got away from shed with a full tender only after the shed labourers, with buckets, had robbed the tenders of the other engines in the hope that the water supply would start flowing later and give a supply for those robbed. Engines' tenders were well filled at West Drayton in the evenings as an insurance against a lack of water on Paddington shed. One of the shed labourers at Paddington was an eighteen-year-old Londoner, Charlie Weller, who had been a stoker on a Thames river steamer plying from Sheerness to The Pool for two years before he joined the Great Western in 1838 as their first engine cleaner. He was a typical cockney, small, energetic and cheerful, often singing a song – he wrote his own words – just the sort of man Seymour Clarke needed when the Great Western Railway was getting by on human bucket chains and hand pumps.

1839 came in frozen solid; on 4 and 8 January the shed tank remained empty all night, the canal being frozen at the sluice. Clarke rose to the occasion by filling the eight o'clock engine's tender by buckets of water taken from the other engines while Charlie and another man took the Company's fire engine round to a well near Seymour Clarke's cottage to fill the appliance's tank by the bucketful, raised on the windlass of the garden well. The trains were late leaving Paddington that morning, and when the immediate crisis had been overcome with well-water, Clarke got his men to dig a deep sump in an old saw pit within the boundary of the shed which he suspected of harbouring a spring. Sure enough the pit flooded to the brim, a hand pump was fitted and the old saw pit formed an emergency water supply until the canal thawed.

Locomotive water from a saw pit! It summed up the nadir of the railway but the thunderous, black clouds had a silver lining. The Directors had asked Gooch to report – without fear or favour – on what was wrong with the locomotive fleet and on how best to put matters right. Gooch was reluctant to criticise his Chief, but his professional opinion had been requested, he gave it and for a brief moment he fell into Brunel's disfavour but not for long. Brunel could see whose engines performed the best and by September 1839 the next of a long line of fine engines – the 'Star' class and the 'Firefly' class – made their appearance on Great Western metals – both types being to Gooch's inspired designs.

In the meantime they had to struggle on and in March an old nuisance reappeared. Dionysius Lardner was back on the line boldly using Great Western engines, carriages and men in a vain attempt to prove himself right and Brunel wrong. Brunel had no time to waste in refuting the pseudo-scientific nonsense of the Doctor so he asked Charles Babbage to make a study of the track and locomotives. Babbage set out to discover just what the first railway Doctor was doing and so went along to Hanwell station with his eldest son Herschel one Sunday in March 1839, a day so cold and windy that Babbage senior had wound a length of blue, woollen cloth around himself over his top coat. They found Lardner's test train at the station, facing west, with the Sage himself, blue nosed upon the engine. Coupled behind was a coach to shelter an assistant with some device for measuring speed – Babbage said later that Lardner's instruments were such that they would bring discredit upon the soundest cause – and behind the coach were some trucks. The Doctor was hoping to uncouple a truck when a known velocity was reached and to measure the time it took to come to a stand but the man who was to have performed the uncoupling had – not surprisingly – gone sick and the experiment was therefore unable to take place. But now the Babbages had arrived. Far from being embarrassed at being face to face with the man who had helped to expose his earlier nonsense, Lardner had the nerve to ask Babbage to help – not from the shelter of a carriage but out in the gale, standing in the last truck to perform the uncoupling as required.

What Lardner hoped to prove from this manoeuvre Babbage was not sure; the time taken for the wagon to stop would depend rather on whether it was free-wheeling into or with the westerly gale that was howling across the Brent valley. Considerably amused and with the germ of an idea growing in his head, Babbage senior climbed into the last wagon and his son followed. The train set off westwards, into the wind; Lardner's assistant waved from the carriage when the desired velocity had been attained; the Doctor told his driver to ease-up; the couplings slacked-off; Babbage threw the chain off the hook; and Lardner, urging his driver on to give the free-wheeling trucks a clear run, fled a considerable distance westwards down the line. The truck was quickly brought to a stand at the west end of Hanwell viaduct, 65 ft above the valley in the very eye of the gale, and no sooner had it stopped than it began to move, almost impercep- tibly, eastwards. Charles Babbage was already unrolling his length of broad cloth and handed one end to his son. 'Hold it up, Herschel,' he commanded. 'The good Doctor's atmospherics shall make his wagon vanish.' Under the makeshift sail the truck made a fair speed eastwards, back across the viaduct and they were well up the line when Lardner returned, looking about the place where the wagon should have been and peering over the parapet into the chasm below searching for the vanished truck.

Babbage's own test train consisted of the engine, several trucks loaded with pig iron and a closed 2nd class carriage next to the engine which had been gutted and refitted as a dyna- mometer-cum-track-recording car with self-inking pens marking moving rolls of paper to record speed, drawbar pull and vertical and lateral shaking of the carriage at its centre and both ends. He designed the whole machine himself at a cost to himself of £300 and with it carried out tests over five months with his son and three other men for assistants. Running his train at high speed during the week resulted in several near-miss situations so Babbage asked Brunel if he could run at night but this was far more dangerous for the line was more crowded after dark as the contractors carried out the work of removing the redundant piles and of ballasting the track. Drivers were few, the work continuous. After a day driving or firing passenger trains the men would be required to work long into the night either on the engineering trains or in the shed to repair and prepare the engines for the next day's service. Rarely did a man get a full night's sleep and Babbage noted that 'the men were thoroughly overworked'. It took superhuman effort to get the Great Western off the ground.

North Star was allocated to run Babbage's train which was booked out very early, before passenger services started but after the ballast trains had come in, the engine being placed first in the shed to be able to leave first thing in the morning. During the night engineering trains came and went haphazardly and in the darkness Switchman Constable Goodlad walked the tracks at the Westbourne end of Paddington layout, turning the points as required. An up ballast train of twenty-five wagons, each carrying two men, approached; he walked out to meet it, to see which route was required, but the enginemen were asleep and the points from up main to engine shed lay set for the shed. The ballast train trundled into the shed siding and crashed into the line of locomotives – *North Star* leading, putting her once more out of action for six weeks. The enginemen were not hurt beyond being bruised and somewhat roughly shaken out of a deep sleep.

Only after this did it occur to Babbage that he might 'without impropriety avail myself of the repose of Sunday for advancing my measures'. His recording equipment broke down on several occasions in the early days of the trials but the breakdowns served to show up bad design; Babbage remedied the faults and soon the entire machine performed perfectly. One evening Charles Babbage, Herschel and the three assistants were travelling in the test coach, coming up from Maidenhead. They stood around the long table across which was sliding, at 4 ft to the mile, 1000 ft of paper, and a dozen pens, fixed to a bridge across the centre of the table, were tracing their information, graphlike, onto it as a roll of blotting paper dried the trace before the paper coiled onto the far spool.

The five men watched in silence under the light of four argand lamps as their six-wheeled carriage 'dagga-dummed' through the dark and the pens marked by slow curves or sharp little jumps the course that the rails dictated. The bright lights prevented any sight of the outside scene and Babbage senior asked if anyone knew where they were. No one answered and they continued to watch the pens. Suddenly two pens made a

familiar, distinctive squiggle. They all looked at Charles, and
Herschel, with a broad grin, said: 'Thames Junction.' This was
where a little railway called the Bristol, Birmingham & Thames
Junction crossed the Great Western on the level at right angles,
about three miles west of Paddington. As a result of this experience Babbage suggested that some device similar to what he
had been using, but simplified, might be placed on the engine to
show the driver where he was in thick fog and also suggested a
'self-registering means of the engine recording its own velocity'.
For use *after* a crash, to provide valuable information about
the last seconds *before* an accident, he specified a clockwork
recorder – a Victorian 'black box' to be fitted to all trains as
a way of discovering what went wrong when some disaster
occurred. Neither he nor Brunel nor Gooch suggested the
obvious – better brakes.

Babbage went to Paddington one Sunday, collected his
official guide and went with him to the engine shed to collect the
engine, *Atlas,* and attach it to the test train of dynamometer car
and three, heavily laden open trucks. His guide told him that as
a result of engineering work on the down line they would go out
on the up line where they could work until 5 p.m. when the first
up train would be due. Babbage was concerned to know by
what authority they were to proceed *down* the up line and
questioned the wisdom of the procedure. The man assured him
and at last he was convinced and down the up line he resolved to
go. But then there was a delay. *Atlas* was late getting up steam
and while they were waiting a message came that the down line
was now clear and they could run on that for the rest of the day.
Babbage's guide, who was probably fed up with coming out
early on his only day off, said grumpily, 'It would not matter
which road we used, both are perfectly clear until five tonight.'
But Babbage, whose ears had become 'peculiarly sensitive to
the sound of an engine', now told his brain that one engine was
approaching. He informed his railway guide. 'Sir – it is impossible,' snapped the official.

'Impossible or not,' replied Babbage, 'there is one coming

and we shall soon see its steam.'

Into view came an engine, the guide's face reddened and both men hurried to the points where the engine would have to turn into the shed. Who should get down off the engine but Brunel, covered in soot and smuts.

'What brings you here?' asked Babbage, as they shook hands.

'I posted up from Bristol to Maidenhead hoping to catch a train but found only this engine with its fire in and steam up so I ordered it out and have driven up at fifty miles per hour.'

Babbage informed him that, but for *Atlas* being late, he would have been in head-on confrontation with the test train running at 40 mph with 90 tons of pig-iron in tow. 'And what would you have done then?' asked Babbage.

Brunel, airy as ever on this sort of subject, said jokingly, 'I should have put on all the steam I could command with a view to driving you off the road by my superior velocity.'

FIVE

Barbarous Structures

Brunel was a fair-minded man, friendly towards his sub-
ordinates but always 'in charge' – the cutting edge there if
necessary. When Driver John Hill came up from Slough to
Paddington in record time the Directors fined him for speeding
but Brunel went to the shed, gave him the sovereign – and asked
what was so special about his engine. Brunel's rebukes were
first given in tones of hurt surprise – that the person could have
let him down – and if the hint was not taken he became curt and,
very rarely, downright abusive. One assistant who had been
ignoring the warning signs got a letter from the great man:
'Plain, gentlemanly language seems to have no effect on you. I
must try stronger language and stronger methods. You are a
cursed, lazy, inattentive vagabond and if you continue to
neglect my instructions and to show such infernal laziness I
shall send you about your business.' But he was also prepared
to defend his men against all comers. In 1842, the Directors
complained to Brunel that a certain draughtsman in an office at
Paddington had a pair of boxing gloves hanging on the wall –
they were to be removed. Brunel wrote a stern reply, not
concealing his disgust at such pettiness. 'I do not know why a
gentlemanly and industrious young man like X should have his
trifling actions remarked upon unless the observer gives him
credit for a gentler temper than I possess; because I confess, if
any man had taken upon himself to remark upon my going to
the pantomime – which I do every Christmas – no respect
for Directors would have restrained me. I will do my best
to keep my team in order but I cannot do it if the master sits

by me and amuses himself by touching them up with the whip.'

Brunel could also use a splendidly dry sarcasm, as in his reply to Mr Griffiths, the lessee of the dreadful refreshment rooms on Swindon station. Griffiths's manager, Mr Player, had complained about a supposedly derogatory remark Brunel had passed concerning the quality of the coffee sold there. Griffiths wrote to Brunel and got the following reply: 'I assure you, Mr Player is quite wrong in supposing that I thought you purchased inferior coffee. I thought I said to him that I had never tasted such bad roasted corn. I did not think you had such a thing as coffee in the place.'

When the new factory at Swindon needed a water supply, Brunel wrote to the management of the Wilts & Berks canal – which passed along the boundary of the works – asking to borrow 20,000 to 30,000 gallons a day. The canal people thought they were onto a good thing and said they would supply – at 3d per gallon per day. 'My dear Sir,' came back Brunel's shocked reply, 'I only want to borrow the water – borrow it and return it somewhat warmer than I took it.'

On 5 August 1840 Brunel was travelling in the three o'clock up train from Faringdon Road (Challow), due into Paddington at 5.20 p.m. but which passed the Scrubbs (Old Oak Common) behind a failing engine at 6.45. A 'light' engine sent out from Paddington to search for the errant train passed it at the Scrubbs and promptly reversed to run up the down line, pacing the staggering engine of the passenger train and getting back into the terminus five minutes after the 7 p.m. was due to have left. Luckily the policeman had remembered that the search engine would be returning 'wrong road' and had held the 7 p.m. until the engine had arrived.

Brunel's anxiety had increased as seven o'clock came and went, sitting in the crawling, up train, imagining a three-train pile-up and reported the incident to the Board. Gooch was in Newcastle, examining some new engines so the Directors called in his assistant, Mr Andrews, for an explanation.

'Oh, that is not my province,' exclaimed Andrews. 'You must speak to Mr Sturrock.'

'Sturrock? Who is Mr Sturrock?' asked the Directors.

'Mr Archibald Sturrock – Mr Gooch's new assistant,' replied Andrews with much secret satisfaction at being able to slip out of the row whilst making it worse for his replacement.

The Directors were astonished and Brunel penned one of his curt letters to Gooch. 'Let me know directly you get home. I find several things in the Locomotive Department unsatisfactory. On Sunday last the Directors sent for Andrews for an explanation of some arrangements of the engines and he, Andrews, was surprised to be considered responsible but referred to a Mr Sturrocks, or some such name. Now he may or may not be a proper person and Andrews may or may not have proved himself efficient but it cannot be right that a man whose name I nor the Directors have ever heard of and who, to the best of my knowledge, I never saw before should be appointed to any responsible position. I should not have done it without the Directors' sanction but that is a matter between me and them – you must look to me. A practical evil has resulted, the probable consequences of which I am frightened to think. Great attention is needed in the management of our staff, in their regulation and discipline but not in the economical management of our engines which is excellent.'

It was a formidable letter to come home to but it all turned out right in the end. Sturrock, so informally appointed, survived to become first Works Manager at Swindon and, later, Locomotive Superintendent of the Great Northern Railway. Dan Gooch eventually became Sir Dan, Chairman of the Great Western Board.

Brunel let nothing pass his notice as he travelled between London and his great feats of engineering in the west and always found time to write a simple note to correct or improve matters. On 6 October 1841 he wrote to Gooch suggesting that all GWR engines should carry, in addition to the usual, fairly high-pitched whistle, a very deep-toned whistle to be the driver's signal to the guard when he needed the train's brake applied. The new whistles were very quickly fitted for on 31 October Brunel again wrote to Gooch complaining that he had heard some brake whistles not as deep toned as he required and asking him to set the matter right.*

After Brunel had brought the driving of Box tunnel to a successful conclusion – a hole almost two miles long through some very hard rock – and might justifiably have thought the matter was behind him, his work was attacked by another of the doctors who have plagued the railway. Doctor William Buckland, a highly respected geologist, at a lecture at the Institution of Civil Engineers, gave it as his eminent opinion that the Bath stone and millstone grit rocks would collapse when trains passed through the tunnel owing to their vibrations and to 'concussions of the atmosphere'. It was a curiously Lardneresque attack and produced a scare right through the Letters columns of *The Times*. Brunel wearily took up his pen and wrote a gently sarcastic note to Buckland, saying that, while he regretted his lack of a scientific knowledge of geology, he had had some recent experience of excavating the rock in question and there was no possibility of it falling down. Buckland had never been near the tunnel.

On 9 April each year, Brunel's birthday, the sun rises just right to shine through the tunnel before it could be seen over the hill and, before smoke blackened the fresh-cut stone, the interior shone like gold in the red, morning sunlight.

With Box tunnel complete it was possible to open the Bath to Chippenham section and thereby open throughout from Paddington to Bristol and on to Bridgwater on the Bristol & Exeter Railway. The auspicious occasion was advertised for 30 June 1841 – somewhat prematurely as it turned out because when Sir Frederick Smith, for the Board of Trade, inspected the new section he found so much work incomplete that he refused to

---

*British Railways Western Region were still fitting these whistles in 1950 and today you can hear them on various preserved locomotives.

sanction it as safe for public use. After some intense, even desperate, haggling he relented and gave permission for the public opening on condition that Gooch and Saunders personally supervised the working of trains.

The first train, an inspection special, ran up from Bath to Chippenham behind *Meridan,* driven by Cuthbert Davison with Brunel on the footplate. *Meridan* and her sister engine, *Fireball,* had been shipped to Bristol docks from Newcastle and Liverpool respectively where they had been met by Davison and Bob Roscoe, the latter a Liverpool man who had been encouraged in his real enthusiasm for steam engines by Jim Hurst. Roscoe and Davison supervised the engines' removal, on special trolleys, along the Bath road to Saltford and, in the railway tunnel there, set up a workshop to bring the engines into full operational condition. Box tunnel was lit throughout its 1¾ mile length by thousands of candles while the navvies finished their work and *Meridan* was half a mile into the flickering, glittering interior when some workmen came running down towards her waving 'Danger'. Davison quickly brought his train to a stand just a few feet short of the end of the up line – the up main line of the Great Western Railway had not yet been completed.

Brunel rapidly got the men organised. In the flickering gloom of that candle-lit cavern he helped to slew the up line into the down line, a set of points was made on the spot and four hours after going into the tunnel on the up line it emerged at the opposite end on the down line and proceeded to Chippenham without further incident where the first public train was waiting the 'All Clear'. It left with Daniel Gooch on the footplate acting as pilotman for the section of single line in the tunnel, the policeman at each end having orders to let no train enter the tunnel unless Gooch was riding on the engine. All that day and late into the night Gooch went to and fro with each train. At 11 p.m. he was riding on the engine of an up train inside the tunnel when he saw a green light on the track ahead – in those days all GWR trains carried one green headlight. Gooch looked at it disbelievingly for a moment then ordered the train to be reversed. The train jolted to a stand, the passengers getting a severe tumbling, it reversed and shot backwards out of the tunnel and came to a stand in Box station – which, fortunately, was not occupied by a train – the down train following too close for comfort but just managing to stop without colliding. Gooch got the down train out of the way and took his train back into the tunnel only to suffer the indignity of having his engine jump the rails deep inside the big hole. For a full forty-eight hours Gooch maintained this duty and experienced much of the hardships of the locomotivemen – except that he was kept well supplied with good food and drink by the ever-thoughtful Brunel.

So the line was opened from Paddington to Bridgwater but the Great Western was uniquely inept in the handling of its customers – though the 1st class fared better than the rest. The Bristol to Bridgwater section was owned by the Bristol & Exeter Company independent of the GWR and passengers for stations west of Bristol who bought their tickets from GWR stations frequently found themselves stranded on Bristol station, the GWR train having missed the B&ER connecting service.

Passengers arriving at Paddington found lawns of fresh-laid turf set with flower beds bordering the gravel drive and smooth, stone pavement leading up to the new, white bricks of Bishop's Road bridge which formed the station offices. It looked very smart, but the Company's police were hard-pressed to defend flowers and were ruthless in their prosecution of flower poachers. To the many impoverished urchins of west London the flowers were just so many posies to be harvested and sold. Chief Inspector Collard found two ten-year-old girls each with a handful of wallflowers and arrested them, putting them into the custody of the station's 'housekeeper', Mary Counsell. They were detained in her office for ten minutes, given a ticking-off and allowed to go. Next day Collard found himself pilloried in the Letters columns of *The Times* for 'imprisoning little children'.

A short distance from Paddington station stood a public house called the Mint, built in the lanes not too close to anything

much, a year before the Great Western Railway had even
been proposed. The landlord of the place was therefore delighted
when his rural pub turned into a cross between a coaching inn
and a terminus café overnight – haunted by cabbies waiting for
fares; thronged with travellers buying a tot to steady their
nerves before, or after a train journey; and frequented by railwaymen who got tipsy and went back to the station where they
were impertinent to the passengers and with fuddled hands
dropped trunks from the roofs of carriages. The Great Western
Directors were far from delighted and stationed a policeman on
the gate of the pub to prevent railwaymen from entering and, to
balance the publican's loss of trade, allowed him to send beer
but not spirits into the Company's stables for two hours each
day for distribution to the men. The compromise did nothing to
reduce the number of inebriated porters though it did increase
the number of inebriated policemen so the Great Western
bought the lease of the pub and converted it into a coffee tavern.

New, alcohol-serving taverns sprang up; the population of
Paddington grew more in five years, 1838–43, than in the
preceding thirty; a 'boom town' grew up around the station
which became rather lawless – 'out in the sticks' beyond west
London – so the Directors called in extra help, from God. A new
church was built to the neo-gothic designs of Thomas Cundy
and in 1845 St Mary's, Paddington (surely it ought to have been
St Christopher?) was opened for the edification of all those
wishing to contemplate the hereafter before boarding a Great
Western train and for the civilising of every possible railwayman.

The Great Western liked to have its business well organised
and not just its own servants; the passengers, too, were supervised or bullied by the liveried railwaymen using a set of
regulations quite unlike those in use on any other railway and
considered by the public to be utterly un-English and tyrannical.

In the 1840s the GWR was truly 'a rich man's railway' as
Gooch stated later in his *Diaries*. Only 1st class passengers were
encouraged, 2nd class were tolerated in the hope of their being
pressured into travelling 1st next time, while the 3rd class were

allowed into Great Western train only after dark and were conveyed in coal trucks in goods trains – furthermore, they were prohibited from carrying more than 14 lb of luggage and, according to the Rule of that time, 'No member of the staff may give assistance to 3rd class passengers'. Yet for all this snobbery the 1st class traveller, on arrival at Paddington in his private conveyance, surrounded by his friends, chattels and servants, was taken in charge by railwaymen – diddled, docketed and directed by members of the lower orders, men who, if they had travelled, would have gone 3rd class – men who were merely servants of the Great Western Railway but, by Act of Parliament, were also Dictators of the Passengers, a most unnatural reversal of the order of things, detested by everyone except the railwaymen. Each passenger had his ticket hand-written by the booking clerk, giving date, destination and train. Children under three travelled free, all other passengers paid full fare but it was not long before the Directors directed that even babies were to pay. The public protested in the best way they could as this letter from Seymour Clarke to Charles Saunders shows:

> The late order about infants is, I fear, doing us much harm . . . Judge Pattison came with his family today, his fare amounting to 40 shillings, and upon demand being made for his infant he at once ordered horses and posted.'Others have also gone by coach.

This was a serious matter and on 10 April 1839 it was decreed that infants could go free and children up to ten at half-price. With his hand-written ticket the passenger went to the platform where a policeman examined it and referred him to the guard or conductor of the train to be placed by one of these gentlemen in a compartment of the official's choice. There was no appeal against the sentence if the passenger disliked the look of the company, nor could those already seated object to who was being introduced. Never before had English people of the sort then travelling been subjected to such regulation; neither would they have been on any other railway.

The first vehicle behind the engine's tender was an open-sided 2nd class carriage into which – at Paddington at any rate – were placed the 'bodies' (as the passengers were known to the staff) for all stations to Slough. Next came a very heavy luggage van made entirely of iron, a most intimidating vehicle quite capable of crushing the leading carriage in the not unlikely event of the train crashing into a stationary train ahead and which, in any case, continuously buffeted the leading carriage as the train ran or braked. When young Queen Victoria travelled on the Great Western her carriage was placed third, behind two of these massive vans with two more behind to protect the rear and the public drew the inference that the Great Western knew perfectly well how most safely to marshal a train but deliberately chose not to do so in order to pressure 2nd class passengers into going 1st.

Each train between 1840–3 had a crew of six or seven: driver, fireman, front and rear guards, conductor and one or two boys who helped the 1st class travellers. The conductor was nominally in charge of the train and was supposed to ride on the engine to supervise the handling of the machine and to ensure that the driver did not get too drunk – conductors were very superior persons and wore smart 'civilian' clothes. The atmosphere on the footplate with such a person present can easily be imagined – the pugnacious Jim Hurst or surly Harry Appleby taking instruction in engine driving from an untrained supernumerary in civilian clothes. The conductors usually rode with the senior guard and by 1845 the grade had been abolished, the men going as ticket collectors in many cases.

When the passengers had all been safely locked away the train could start. The Company took several years to learn to trust its passengers – and to get fences up around the stations so as to prevent the escape of ticketless travellers. The conductor had his waybill, the 'bodies' were stacked like parcels in definite compartments according to their destination and when the train stopped he let those passengers out who were booked to alight. No call of nature, no hunger or thirst would sway him –

the boys fetched refreshment to parched or frozen 1st class travellers – a passenger had a ticket to a particular destination and that was where he was let out.

The open 2nd class carriages cost the traveller two-thirds of the 1st class fare but the danger and discomfort of riding in them was immeasurably greater than in the 1st class so that those who could pay the bit extra were tortured into doing so while those who could not were merely tortured. One passenger returned to the Directors a piece of cinder with the following note:

> Gentlemen,
> I really think you ought to take some remedy to prevent dust and burning cinders flying in the faces of persons travelling by your conveyance. I am at present suffering much inconvenience from dust being blown into my eyes and from the enclosed cinder which fell within my shirt collar in a burning state and caused a large blister to rise. Had it landed in my eye it would have deprived me of sight.

The Great Western frequently set itself public deadlines for improving them but the carriages ran for at least seven years without alteration. Fires from falling cinders or from over-heated axle bearings were a constant source of worry to the locked-in passengers. On 8 May 1842, for example, a train caught fire at Versailles burning to death fifty-three locked-in travellers. The British travelling public – and especially the Great Western's locked-in clientele – were appalled; one might have thought that the Company would have abandoned the practice but it did not and a month after the French tragedy the Reverend Sydney Smith, clergyman of that literary village, Combe Florey, turned his famous wit broadside upon the Directors – with a swide-swipe at Bishops, Monopolies and Anglo-Catholic Dr Pusey in passing – in a series of letters to the *Morning Chronicle* which could be summarised thus:

> It seems to me perfectly monstrous that a board of ten monopolists

can read such a description as that of the Versailles fire and say to
the public, 'You must take your chance of being burnt or mutilated.
We have arranged our plan upon the locking-in principle and we
shall not incur the expense of changing it.' Their plea is that rash or
drunken people will attempt to get out of the carriage while it is in
motion if it is not locked so that the lives of two hundred persons,
who are not rash or drunk, are to be endangered for the half-yearly
preservation of some idiot – upon whose body the Coroner is to sit –
and over whom the sudden death man will deliver his sermon
against the Directors. The fact of locking the doors will be a
frequent source of accidents – whatever the Directors think –
mankind is impatient of combustion. The passengers will attempt
to escape through the windows and ten times more mischief will be
done than if they had been left to escape through the doors. The
public have a right to every advantage under a monopoly which
they would enjoy under free enterprise. If there were two parallel
railways, the one locking in and the other not, is there any doubt as
to which would carry away the traffic? Can there be any hesitation
in which timid women, drunken men, sages, Bishops and all com-
bustible beings would place themselves? I arrive by train at a
station, others are admitted but I am forbidden to leave though
perhaps at the point of death. In life there is ingress and egress
except between Paddington and Bridgwater where even Habeas
Corpus is refused. Why are there no strait-jackets? Why is the
traveller not strapped down? I do not recall being tied to the
outside of a stage-coach. In ships landsmen are not locked in their
cabins to prevent them falling overboard. Is it to save a few fellow
creatures or a few pounds that the Children of the West are to be
hermetically sealed in locomotives? Railroad travelling is a delightful improvement in human life. The Mama rushes sixty miles in
two hours to the aching finger of her conjugating and declining
grammar boy, the early Scotsman scratches himself in the mists of
the north and has his porridge in Piccadilly before the setting sun.
The Puseyite priest, after a rush of one hundred miles, appears
before his bookseller with his little book of nonsense before break-
fast. But we must not close our eyes to the price we shall pay for
this. Every three or four years there will be a massacre – 300 killed
on the spot – the newspapers all up in arms – a great combustion of
human bodies – then a thousand regulations forgotten as soon as

the Directors dare. The first person of rank to be killed will put everything in order. I hope it will not be a Bishop but should it be so let the burnt Bishop, the unwilling Latimer, remember that, however painful gradual concoction by fire may be, his death will produce unspeakable benefit to the public.

Sydney Smith lived towards the end of that time when a man might become famous, the friend of great men, on the strength of his wit alone – he died in 1845. When the Prime Minister, Lord John Russell, went down to see him at Combe Florey he found oranges tied to Smith's apple trees and a very confused donkey wandering the garden with a set of deer antlers fixed to its head, the Reverend Smith believing that this would make Lord John feel he was in the Holy Land rather than Somerset.

Clergymen were ever eccentric. The incumbent of Dowlish Wake, near Illminster, in 1845 was Ben Speke, brother of the famous explorer. The Reverend Speke was seen taking the London train at Taunton one day and was seen later at Paddington but he then disappeared, his family hearing nothing from him for many weeks. A hue and cry was raised. *The Times* made his fate the subject of editorials – it was all quite perfectly disgraceful. In the eighth week the wanderer was discovered in Padstow, disguised as a cowherd. *Punch*, in announcing the news, said his behaviour was 'un-speke-able'.

However, to return to Great Western Railway 2nd class carriages: Sydney Smith's letters may have had some good effect because shortly after the last one was published the Board of Trade ordered the Great Western to leave at least one door open on each compartment – so the Directors ordered the off-side door to remain unlocked and – to spite the public who had forced this concession from the Company – they made it a rule that no one other than a ticket-carrying passenger could enter any of their stations. Instantly the London papers were full of pathetic or indignant letters detailing the effects of the ban. Here is one from *The Times*, 22 June 1841:

Regarding the tyrannical regulations which prevents friends of

travellers from accompanying them to the train. I escorted a lady
to Paddington ticket office and was compelled to leave her at the
entrance surrounded by a mob through which she had to pass to
join her train in total ignorance of the company with whom she
would be travelling. I was not even allowed to see that her luggage
was secure. Near the end of her journey she fainted and the
gentleman meeting her – not being allowed onto the platform – had
no idea of her plight and, but for the kindness of a perfect stranger,
I do not know what would have been the outcome. This extremely
annoying regulation is not practised by any other company neither
does any other line lock doors on trains.

A month later, after a dozen similar letters to *The Times*, the
Directors relented and allowed onto their station bona-fide
friends and/or servants but no 'idlers or ruffians'.

Passengers' fears of the long journeys – and it was at least
an eighty-minute journey from Paddington to Reading which
might well be performed in total darkness – were not ground-
less: carriages often filled with smoke from burning grease in
overheating axle-boxes and the passengers' cries of alarm were
usually answered with ribaldry from the staff. 'Swells, ruffians
and blackguards' often occupied the compartments into which
others were forced, who then terrorised respectable folk by their
mere presence and sometimes by outright violence. On Tuesday
12 July 1842 a large party of 'swells, nobs and fancy men' with a
strong contingent of pickpockets, the 'sweepings of St Giles and
Whitechapel', were loaded into a train at Paddington to go
down to Twyford to attend a prize fight in the station yard
between one Jones and a character called 'Tom the Greek'. The
rules were simple – bare fists and the last man standing to take
the purse of £50. The fight, though illegal, was well advertised,
crowds came from all parts but the civil authorities did nothing
at all to prevent it. The awful battering match lasted two hours
three minutes before 'Tom the Greek' was knocked to the
cobbles of the yard for the last time and Jones was declared the
winner. Neither men had really won, only the swells, nobs and
fancy men – and the pickpockets. Both boxers' eyes were com-

pletely closed, their heads were horribly swollen. Indeed, the winner's facial injuries were such that he had to be carried to the train in great agony, his head completely covered in a towel which dripped blood on the platform. 'Tom the Greek' was close to death and expired later at his trainer's pub in Windsor.

The Great Western 2nd class carriages were lethal in bad weather having no closed-in sides or partitions closing off each compartment from floor to roof; the wind, rain, snow and hail blew in and through at over 40 mph. The Company promised to improve the carriages by December 1844. In November that year a train left Paddington in the teeth of a westerly storm and in half an hour the floor of each 2nd class carriage was flooded inches deep and the passengers were, quite literally, soaked to the skin. They tried to erect umbrellas but the force of the storm and the train's slipstream turned them inside-out and one elderly man had his torn right out of his numb grasp but the worst was yet to come; to keep their feet out of the flood they were obliged to put them up on the opposite seat – perfect strangers had to sit facing each other 'in the attitude of American cads and loungers'. The railwaymen at Reading and Didcot found it highly amusing to see the bedraggled people all sitting with their feet up, holding inside-out umbrellas, and barely concealed their mirth. 'It's no worse than sitting outside on a stage coach,' they said. But it was, because of the greater speed of the train.

The Company's deadline passed without improvement and in a letter to *The Times* a doctor condemned the GWR 2nd class carriages as 'barbarous structures, disgraceful to our times and country'. Can the reader imagine a journey of several hours – even one hour – sitting in an open coach on a bitterly frosty or soaking wet day? On 21 January 1845 a man travelled 2nd class from Paddington to Bath to take up a fresh position as a servant in a house. The temperature was well below freezing during the journey and when the guard came to let him out at Bath he could see he was frozen rigid and close to death. Calling a porter to help, he lifted the man out of the train, carried him out of the station and dumped him down on the pavement, propped against a wall where he died a few minutes later. The inquest jury passed its verdict: 'Met his death from cold due to severe exposure in a GWR 2nd class carriage', and this was neither the first nor the last time that such a verdict was given.

In March 1845 John Johnathan, a wire-worker already in poor health, took a train from Bristol to Bath in a 3rd class 'carriage' and was so frozen at Bath after only forty-five minutes on the journey that he, too, was carried off the premises and was left to die on the pavement – the important point being that he did not die on Great Western property. The verdict of that jury was: 'Died by visitation of God, his death accelerated by his exposure to the inclemency of the weather in one of the 3rd class carriages of the GWR.'

In January 1845 another passenger wrote:

> I address you from Oxford, aching and shivering under the accumulated miseries which I have endured in a Great Western 2nd class carriage. I entreat some Director to expose his well-attended person to those concentrated blasts of freezing air and penetrating floods of rain which must be felt to be appreciated. On top of a stage-coach you had your due allowance of wind and water but on rail what nature intended to cover an acre is poured onto one suffering head. I shall return to London by 1st class carriage and if I mistake not, that charming luxury of construction – a 2nd class carriage – has worked its true intent.

Six months later some kind of all-weather protection was given to these carriages.

Guards, policemen, porters and enginemen had to suffer and survive bad weather for anything up to eighteen hours a day – perhaps for weeks on end – in the early days of the railway which may well account for their offhand attitude towards those passengers who happened to be getting a soaking once in a while but when conditions became really bad the men rallied round and did whatever they could for their passengers.

On 18 January 1841 heavy rain began falling over the Thames Valley and continued torrentially for forty-eight hours. The 6 p.m. from Reading to Paddington on the 19th headed eastwards into the pitch-dark night with rain bucketing down and by the time the train cleared Sonning cutting the 2nd class passengers were soaked and frozen to the marrow, the rain slashing into their faces or running down their backs with all the force of the icy slipstream. At Twyford the train stopped and the passengers sat in their clinging, sodden clothing, thankful for the respite from the numbing wind. As they waited, twenty labourers, each with a shovel and a lighted lantern, emerged from the station in a long, clattering line. Their ganger went forward to ride on the engine while the others tramped their heavy boots across the platform to board the train, pushing in among the miserable, waterlogged passengers who gratefully took the opportunity to warm their hands over the oil lamps' hot lids. Ruscombe cutting ahead was flooded by a stream which had changed course and the men were going to re-divert it. The train set off with a jolt and a tug, away from the dim-lit station into the ink-black night, rain drumming thunderously on the all-but-useless roofs of the open-sided carriages. Far into the cutting a policeman standing in the flood, exhausted by the weight of his sodden overcoat and leather top hat, waved 'Danger' with his lantern and brought the train to a stand. The ganger climbed down from the engine and splashed back to the carriages, shouting to his men, urging them down into the flood into action. He was stumbling along when the cutting side became semi-liquid and slid, with a horrible, squelching thump, down onto the track, burying the rails and piling up around the carriages, tilting some of them over. For a minute there was pandemonium in the darkness with the passengers screaming and the ganger shouting for help, engulfed in the mud until his men leaped overboard, helped him free and shouted reassurance to the travellers.

The engine was free of the land-slip so it was uncoupled and driven on to Maidenhead to fetch help, leaving the labourers slogging away hopelessly at the mud with their shovels and the passengers sitting in constant fear of a rear-end collision; they would have de-trained and stood out on the cutting side but there was virtually no cutting side on which to stand. Two hours later a relief train came backing down the up line and stopped just short of the flood. The water, pouring down the cutting side, had scoured the earth away leaving deep water; so the labourers took the passengers onto their shoulders and, St Christopher-like, carried them through the hazardous darkness to the new train. Luggage, too, had to be transferred; the leather straps holding it to the roofs had become swollen and stiff with the rain and were almost impossible to undo but at last the stalwart railwaymen transferred everything to the fresh train which then set off for Paddington. Two miles short of Slough it ran into a landslide. The stability of the broad gauge saved an otherwise fatal derailment; the engine forced its way through and though the train was stuck fast the men uncoupled the engine and ran it ahead to get help. For three hours the people sat, half dead with cold, before a train came rumbling backwards out of the darkness and came to a stand opposite the stranded train. Once again people and luggage had to be transferred and having done this they set off once more. At Slough they got the order 'All Change'. Utterly exhausted, bewildered, sore from wet, chafing clothes, they staggered out onto the platform – weary parents and children too exhausted to do more than whimper – and, wonder of wonders, they were all put into a train composed entirely of 1st class carriages as a rare, official gesture of sympathy from the Company. They finished their gruesome journey at 3.15 a.m. at Paddington, having taken 9¼ hours to come from Reading.

SIX

Reckless, Cool and Genial

Daniel Gooch prospered as the Locomotive Superintendent of the Great Western Railway and in 1865 became Chairman of the Board when he was also involved in laying the first, transatlantic cable – for which feat he was given a knighthood. Most of the 'Gooch Originals' – the men who had come south with him as engine drivers – became Foremen or were given plum jobs not only because they were highly capable, hand-picked men but also because they were close friends of the great man; men who had stood loyally by him in the early years when the going was rough, men who had kept the wheels turning when, by rights, those wheels ought not to have turned at all. The exception to this rule was Gooch's oldest friend – Jim Hurst. Jim had been a friend to Gooch since the latter's apprentice days; Driver Jim had taught young Dan, and young Dan Gooch, when he rose in the world, remembered Jim, brought him onto the Great Western and shared his cottage with him at West Drayton. They were close enough to share private jokes and, but for Jim's pugnacious nature, Gooch would have ensured he did well. As it was, Jim took on the role of an engine driver prima donna; he had started on railways with George Stephenson, he was the Great Western's 'Number One' driver and no one was allowed to forget it. It took all of Gooch's influence just to keep Jim in his job on occasions.*

* 'The most essential personal qualifications of an engineman or fireman are: sobriety, steadiness, presence of mind, constant watchfulness on duty. Every man should be able to read and write and understand the mechanism of the locomotive. To have been a locomotive fitter is an advantage. Every man must

Harry Appleby, by contrast, was a dour Geordie, the regular driver of *North Star* from 1839 and he detested Jim for his Lancashire brag and his 'I'm the King of the Castle' manners. Jim thought Harry was a surly oaf and said so and each man tried to sabotage the other's efforts or tried to make him look silly – though they usually contrived to make this look like practical joking. Gooch took Jim's side and got tired of Appleby's constant complaints about Jim's outrages. One day in 1840, Gooch was riding with Jim on the footplate of *Vulcan* going down, out of Paddington, when they saw *North Star* approaching on the up line. Gooch, the Locomotive Superintendent, crouched down out of sight and said to Jim, 'Now Hurst, give Appleby some steam as you pass.' Jim needed no greater encouragement and as *North Star* came by he opened *Vulcan*'s steam cocks. It was the equivalent of blowing the most enormous raspberry and Harry Appleby, enveloped in a cloud of shrieking, clammy steam, furiously took the hint. Back at West Drayton shed that evening he strode up to Gooch, quite unaware that it was he who had been the instigator of the outrage, and demanded justice: 'Either he goes or I do.' To which the youthful Superintendent replied, 'Those who give a joke must learn to take one too, Appleby.'

One day in October 1840 Jim had *Vulcan* out on the line, illegally pumping water into its boiler by driving down the up main, tender first at high speed, when *Wildfire* appeared on its lawful occasion hauling an up passenger train. In the inevitable smash, *Vulcan*'s tender was destroyed; *Wildfire*'s frames were splayed wide open; Jim's fireman took a header off the engine and broke his leg, but Jim survived without a scratch and paid a tiny fine for his total disregard for the rules and common-sense

---

devote himself exclusively to the Company's service, attending at such hours as may be appointed and residing wherever he may be required. Pay is on a weekly basis and for as many hours as may be necessary. Every man to appear in white fustian clothes (corduroy) on the first working day of each week.' – from *A Complete Set of Rules and Regulations for the Practical Management of a Locomotive Engine and for the Guidance of Engine Drivers* by John Sewell (1848)

safety precautions. Small wonder, then, if he thought he could do no wrong.

When the railway from Swindon to Cirencester was opened on 31 May 1841, Jim was transferred to Cirencester shed to work between there and Swindon. At Swindon there was a policeman called Burton who sometimes took a turn as guard and who one day found himself in charge of a train from Swindon to Cirencester which was being driven so recklessly, with such scant regard to passengers' comfort on the starts and stops at stations, that he at last took it upon himself to screw on his handbrake, between Minety and Cirencester, to slow down a fairly precipitate journey. This was no more than his duty as guard but up front the driver was Jim Hurst, who felt the train pull back against him and realised that the guard was slowing him down. What impudence! At Cirencester he stormed back along the platform and accused Burton of trying to break the train in half while the guard defended himself stoutly with counter-accusations of Jim's reckless driving. Jim simply had to browbeat everyone who got in his way. In December that year he was at Swindon, waiting to take a train to Cirencester when he discovered that Burton was the guard. Instantly he went into a rage and refused to work the train on the grounds that Burton was a menace to safe working. He defied the Station Master and the Divisional Locomotive Superintendent and generally had a fine old row at the platform's end. They replaced Burton and Jim worked the train but his revenge cost him a £2 fine for delaying the train.

Jim was an unholy terror to work with. At Cirencester he bullied the police and porters into nervous wrecks – he must have been a thorough bore to his fireman. He enjoyed driving fast about the station's sidings so as to make the policeman run hard from one point capstan to the next, all the while shouting abuse at the man. In August 1842 the inevitable happened. Switchman Tom Powell was on duty in Cirencester yard; Jim was making him rush about; Tom failed to turn a certain switch quickly enough; and clever Jim Hurst and his engine took a

short trip down a low embankment. Jim's first priority was to
get his story to the Station Master, John Ashbee, telling him
that Powell was not fit to be in charge of the signalling. Ashbee
was puzzled; Tom Powell seemed to him to be a decent sort, so
Ashbee had him into the office for his side of the story. Powell,
fearing for his job, broke down almost into tears and the whole,
miserable story of Jim Hurst's bullying came out. Powell was
not blamed for what had happened and from that day on the
entire staff of the Swindon to Cirencester line were out to 'get'
Jim Hurst.

Jim gave them plenty of opportunity. He regularly took
passengers on his engine – and not always when it was hauling a
train. After the line to Gloucester had been opened from a
junction with the Cirencester line at Kemble, in 1845, Jim
would use his engine as a taxi and helpfully run passengers
three at a time from Kemble to Cirencester if it happened that
they were in too much of a hurry to wait for the regular train –
and taxi drivers have to be paid. In August 1845, Tom Powell
saw William Bershaw and Isaac Hart arrive at Cirencester on
Jim's engine and saw each man give him a silver coin. Jim
touched his cap and pocketed the money. When they had gone,
Tom said to Jim, 'A shilling is a lot for a ride from Kemble.' To
which Jim Hurst replied, 'That was for more than one trip, they
owed me for other times.'

A report was sent to Chief Inspector Collard and Jim was
summoned to appear before the Board on a charge of allowing
members of the public to ride on his engine, of taking money
from them, and of not handing over the said money to the
Company. The charge was serious so Jim conferred with Daniel
Gooch who recommended testimonial letters from Kershaw
and Hart. Jim duly answered his summons and produced the
letter which testified that, while they had indeed ridden on
Hurst's engine, they had never given him any money.* The

---

* *Hart's Letter to GWR Directors,* 1842
Sir, Having been informed that James Hurst is reported for taking me from

word of the joy-riders was accepted and Jim was posted to
Totnes, so, although the staff of the Cirencester line breathed a
great sigh of relief, Jim Hurst had won again for one could
hardly consider working on bank engines or on the Ashburton
branch as a punishment. From Totnes the requirements of the
service or the punishments of the Directors took him and his
wife to Swansea, Leamington and back to Paddington by 1854.

When Jim moved down to Devon his eldest son, Edward,
started as a cleaner on Swindon shed, became a fireman at
Bristol in 1850 and by 1853 was a driver at Swindon and truly 'a
chip off the old block', following with uncanny precision in his
father's pugnacious path. Jim Hurst junior began as a cleaner
on Brimscombe bank engine shed in June 1852 but, being a
quiet, thoughtful character – perhaps taking after his mother –
he transferred to a Swindon works apprenticeship in 1854,
laboured at the practice and theory of engineering for seven
years and emerged to live a quiet life as Foreman of the Works'
breakdown gang except for a few years spent 'on loan' to the
newly built Jersey Railway as Locomotive Superintendent.

Jim Hurst senior, meanwhile, was careering along, arguing
with all and sundry, making enemies as easily as most men
make friends. In October 1854 he was driving a down train past
the site of what later became Hayes station when the lineside
policeman ventured to express his opinion of Driver Hurst by
throwing a lump of ballast at him. The policeman could not
have given much thought to the consequences of such irrever-
ence. The engine's brake whistle boomed for the guard's brake;
the fireman wound on his hand brake; Jim threw the engine into
reverse and in a few minutes, as the passengers picked themselves up off the floor, he was running back along the line,

---

Cirencester to Ewen and receiving pay for so doing which is not true. I never
rode when he had a train. The last time I rode as near that I can remember
was in April or May. He never made a charge, neither did I ever give him
anything to the truth of which I hereunto set my name, Sept. 6, 1842.

                                                        Isaac Hart

Ewen in the Parish of Kemble.

rolling his shirtsleeves up as he went. Nothing short of a fight would assuage Jim's outraged egotism and he there and then invited the policeman into the adjoining field for a mauling. The bobby very wisely refused and Jim's feelings remained unvented as he stormed back to his engine. However, the guard, unaware of who had cast the first stone and seeing only the dreadful Jim Hurst demanding to fight the policeman – to the great consternation of the passengers – booked the delay and the reasons for it in his journal. The Directors fined Jim 10 shillings for wanting to fight and the policeman £1 for throwing the stone but to even matters up they transferred Jim to the Forest of Dean branch which had just been opened. Poor Mrs Hurst had to uproot herself, pack their belongings and follow her husband to the next crisis.

The branch led north into the coalmining district around Cinderford and Bilson from the main line of the Gloucester to Newport section of the South Wales Railway which was closely connected with the GWR. Passenger trains for the branch started from Newnham, a mile east of the actual junction, and a porter at Newnham began to annoy Jim. He annoyed him for eighteen months until one day, Jim could stand it no longer, got down off his engine and gave him a severe thrashing to the great alarm of everyone on the platform. A report was sent directly to Paddington from F. G. Saunders, Secretary to the South Wales Railway, with a strong recommendation that Jim Hurst be dismissed. F. G. Saunders was a nephew of Charles Saunders, Secretary to the Great Western Railway. Daniel Gooch was absent on some other business. Jim got the sack. When Gooch returned and heard the news he instantly brought Jim back to Paddington and insisted that he be reinstated. He was. The Traffic Department groaned and one officer said, in Jim Hurst's hearing, 'You can do nothing with Hurst, he follows Gooch's orders.' The men of the Traffic Department braced themselves for the onslaught but for over two years nothing reportable happened – till one day in June 1858 when Jim failed to see the bar against him at Faringdon Road (Challow) and crashed into a horse box, wrecking it and damaging his pocket to the tune of £3 – a huge sum for Jim – showing that even Gooch's patience was beginning to wear a little thin.

Three weeks later, on 10 July, he was working a ballast train (no top link jobs for Jim) and was locked inside the down sidings at Taplow with his fireman George Wright, Head Guard Mark Edwards and Under Guard Wilkins. The switchman was John Absolom. It was a sultry evening and Absolom sweated in his heavy uniform and top hat; he had been shunting both with Jim Hurst's ballast train and the 'Fly' goods in the up sidings. An express from Birmingham was due and the up goods was ready to leave but he padlocked the cast-iron stop-block over the siding exit rail and turned his disc on for the fast which, he supposed, would soon show up. Having secured the up line he walked back to his sentry box to replace the up sidings padlock key on its nail and to fetch the key for the down sidings padlock to unlock the block and allow Jim to shunt out onto the down main line. While Absolom walked his beat, following his careful plan, Under Guard Wilkins uncoupled the engine from the ballast wagons and Jim, impatient for the off as ever, yanked open the regulator to send his engine forward so violently that it smashed into and mounted the cast-iron block, broke a driving wheel spring and came to rest on the down main line – derailed. Instantly Jim rounded on Mark Edwards and accused him of having given 'Right Away' but Edwards, coming out of his astonished shock at the antics of Jim's engine, gave as good as he got telling Jim he had been nowhere near the train when the uncoupling took place. Jim then turned on his fireman and blamed *him* for giving him 'Right Away'. Wrong again but that did not stop him writing a report to Gooch blaming everyone except himself.

The Traffic Department saw a chance of getting rid of Hurst and the Taplow Station Master, Mr Beynon, and the London Divisional Civil Engineer, Michael Lane, mounted a massive campaign against him. It needed to be massive for not only were they seeking to dethrone Gooch's favourite driver, they – the mere Traffic Department – were attacking the Locomotivemen.

Mr Beynon wrote the strongest condemnation of Jim Hurst that he could compose; his letter to the Directors stated: 'I believe this matter to have occurred entirely from the perfectly reckless way this driver goes about his work and although I hesitate to say it I do consider him to be perfectly unfit to be in charge of an engine. Our guard Edwards is a steady man and I have never had a complaint against him.' Michael Lane wrote in defence of the Head Guard a broadside of complimentary adjectives: 'Edwards, the ballast guard, is a sober, steady, truthful, smart, careful man.' The result of all this was to produce no more than a drawn battle – such was Gooch's influence with the Board – and neither side had any men punished.

More cocky than ever, Jim pursued his impetuous way. Next year he was fined 14s 3d for the damage he caused to *Dart*, a 'Firefly' class 7-ft 'Single'*, when he rammed her tender with his engine as he went dashing around the station yard at Reading. Still he took no care and a week later he was driving through the station yard at Reading and rammed *Alma*, knocking one buffer off. Now this was something serious. *Alma* was a fairly new 8-ft 'Single', one of the 'Iron Duke' class each one of which was like a child to their designer, Daniel Gooch. Gooch had no difficulty in choosing between one of his children and his favourite engine driver – Jim was fined his largest sum to date, £3 6s 10d.

Jim's dethronement came in August 1862; the cause is not recorded, but in that month he was transferred to Swindon factory as a labourer – according to the Swindon Locomotive Superintendent, James Thompson – or as driver of the Works' shunter, according to Jim, though after his activities in Reading yard it does not seem likely that he would have been trusted in a factory full of new and freshly repaired locomotives. He worked in the factory until May 1876 and retired at sixty-four after

---

* A 'single wheeler' is an engine with a single pair of driving wheels and from the side looks as if it has only one driving wheel.

thirty-eight years' historic and highly colourful service. He received £100 from the Great Western locomotivemen's own Life Assurance organisation – the Mutual Assurance Society – to which all drivers were obliged to contribute and to which the Directors also granted funds; he also received a pension of £1 4s 6d a week of which 6 shillings was an additional grant from the Board, of which Gooch was Chairman, and a cottage – one of the Brunel originals – just outside the factory walls. With no children now to support and a pension equal to the weekly wages of a skilled man with a family, Mr and Mrs Hurst lived out their days in flowery comfort and sent occasional letters to the Board, accompanied with testimonials, asking for a larger pension.

A totally different character was Michael John Almond, a Geordie, who began his career on pumping engines when he was fifteen in 1822, who moved to locomotive work as soon as he was old enough and who came onto the Great Western Railway in 1838/40, probably coming south by sea with the engine he is most often recorded as driving in those days: the Sharp, Roberts' *Lion*. He gives the impression, from reading the old records, of being a very calm, practical man of great alertness – which means great physical stamina – a man who broke world speed records coolly as an everyday matter. He had crashes it is true but with nonexistent brakes and other men's errors he can hardly be blamed and very often his quick action, prompted by sharp, long-distance eyesight, saved fatal accidents from taking place.

On 22 February 1841 Almond was driving *Lion* on the 8.30 a.m. out of Paddington and was just pulling across Hanwell viaduct after the station stop when the engine's valve gear fell to pieces and became entangled in the spokes of the 6-ft diameter driving wheel. The guard ran back to Hanwell station to make sure the policeman kept his bar on to protect the broken-down train while Almond and his fireman examined *Lion* to see if they could make him mobile. When the guard returned they were trying to prise tangled rodding off the wheel using their fire-irons as levers and the conductor was trying to pacify a very agitated passenger in an open 2nd class coach who was worried about missing an important appointment at Southall. The guard told Michael Almond that arrangements had been made to rescue the train and then went back to help with the increasingly irate passenger. The man was standing, leaning with both hands over the side of the carriage, demanding in a loud voice to be let out so that he could walk along the line to Southall.

'It will be perfectly safe, this train is blocking the line and my appointment is most urgent.'

With great satisfaction the guard was able to quash that suggestion. 'But it will not be safe, there is another engine coming to push us.'

'When?' demanded the passenger hopefully.

'In about an hour or so.'

'An hour?!'

The man swung his leg over the side and jumped to the ground. The guard and conductor caught him on the way down and threw him back into the train. As they did so there was a loud explosion and a roar of steam from the engine. Almond had been prising the rodding away when the sharp-ended poker, several feet long, which he was using, slipped and dug into the firebox causing a slight tear which exploded into a large hole. The two train-men ran forward to see and the passenger, seizing his chance, leaped from the train and would have run past them but was intercepted by Michael Almond and his mate.

The man was furious: 'You are guilty of an assault – I shall sue you – let me go.'

The men let go, with a warning: 'You cannot walk along the line.'

Groping inside his greatcoat the passenger produced his card and handed it to the conductor. 'My card,' he snapped. 'I will meet your Company in court if they so wish.' He dodged quickly around the front of the engine, down the high, steep embankment to the field and the main road a few yards away.

Michael Almond had strong nerves, sharp eyes and snake-

1 Daniel Gooch (1816–89) with a model of *Firefly*, the prototype of his standardised express locomotive fleet

2 Jim Hurst (1811–92), Gooch's companion during the latter's apprentice days and the GWR's first driver

3 *Vulcan* (1037–70), the first engine to steam on Great Western metals and Jim Hurst's engine for several years

4 Isambard Kingdom Brunel (1806–59), Chief Engineer of the GWR, leans with
   casual ease against a post while Lord Carlisle (*l*) and Lord Paget sit staring with
   worried frowns at the camera, *c.* 1855

5 The west end of Box tunnel, 1842: the policeman is giving 'All Right' to a down train; overhead the disc is turned 'on' for up trains while the 'Caution' board is 'on' with its green face turned towards up trains

6 Brunellian Baronial for Bristol: Temple Meads station in 1842 with some men pushing a truck loaded with a horse-drawn carriage and a 'Star' about to set out on another epic journey to London over 'the greatest work in England'

7 'The Driver of 1852'
from Fores' *Contrasts*

8 'The Gentleman who was
locked up because he had
lost his Ticket'

9 Chippenham engine shed, *c.* 1848: *Polar Star* (*l*), express engine with 7-ft driving wheels; *Alligator (c)*, 5-ft-wheeled goods engine uncoupled from its tender; *Javelin* (*r*), 6-ft-wheeled 'Small Firefly' passenger engine

10 *Lord of the Isles*, built in March 1851, shown at the Great Exhibition, pride of the Great Western Railway, at Swindon, *c.* 1870

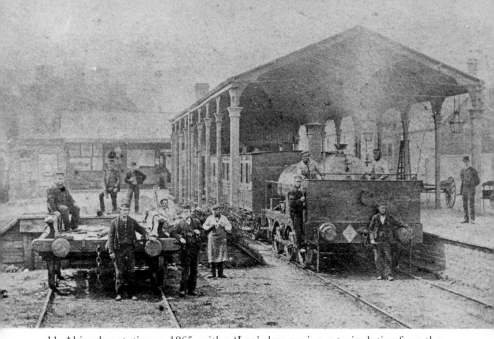

11 Abingdon station, *c.* 1865, with a 'Leo' class engine, a train dating from the 1840s and a jolly crew of railwaymen

12 Wootton Bassett Road station looking east, *c.* 1885. Mixed gauge, signalled by semaphores and electric telegraph under the 'block section' system installed 1874. Signal box on right, beyond a disc-and-crossbar signal acts as 'repeater' for the semaphore; the bar has downward-pointing lugs for the 'down' line

13 Gauge-conversion train and crew of navvies relaxing off-duty, Grange Court, west of Gloucester, August 1869

14 Flood damage to narrow-gauge track south of Oxford, 1875. The train is on the up main, behind it is a disc and crossbar acting as distant signal for the diverging branch line a mile further south

17 Driver G. Eggar with *Inkermann* on the down 'Flying Dutchman' acknowledges the Worle Jc. signalman's white flag which indicates that the line is clear to the next signal box—a survival from the old 'time interval working' days

18 A 'Rover' passing Stoke Canon, July 1890. The signal box is of GWR design built when the Tiverton branch (*extreme left*) was opened on 1 May 1885, the branch semaphore being the modern pattern while that on the main line is the original pattern

19 *Iron Duke* at Bristol, 5 November 1890. The driver has disconnected the
communication cord from the whistle so that it will not interfere with the
Revd A. H. Malan's photograph

20 The junctions at Swindon looking west, *c.* 1880 (*see App. 4*)

21 The common rail changing sides
   (*see App. 4*)

22 Overhead signal wires
   (*see App. 4*)

23 The hoary old signalman of Waltham box, near Maidenhead—veteran of many a bitter winter's night at the foot of a disc-and-crossbar signal—with the permanent-way gang on the steps of his new-fangled signal cabin, *c.* 1890

24 Gwinear Road station soon after the opening of the Helston branch on 9 May 1887. The latest pattern buildings, signal and narrow-gauge engine

25 Sir Daniel Gooch, Bt., MP for Cricklade, Locomotive Superintendent of the
GWR, 1837–64; supervised laying first transatlantic telegraph cable, 1864/5;
Chairman of the Board of the GWR, 1865–89. In February 1889 he told
shareholders that the abolition of the broad gauge could not be long delayed;
he shortly afterwards became ill and died on 15 October 1889

26 Ivybridge station early in 1892 with the ballast pulled aside to allow the transoms to be cut prior to slewing in the outer rail to conform to the width of the 'coal-cart' gauge. The tank engine is ex-South Devon Railway *Lance*, GWR No 2130

27 Millbay Dock station, Plymouth, 21 May 1892. The broad gauge had given Great Western men a feeling of pride. A guard who had been fatally injured on the track by a broad-gauge engine said to the doctor, 'I'm glad it wasn't one o' them narrer-gauge engines as did it'

28 Only the gauge changed—the high quality of the men continued to serve the
Company and the country. A Fairford branch ganger on his velocipede is
photographed near Yarnton Junction, *c.* 1892

swift reactions, necessary reactions for any driver in any age but vital for sheer survival in the 1840s. He was given *Queen* new from Swindon works in March 1846 – a 'single wheeler' engine with 6-ft diameter driving wheels. The technique for shrinking on and keying securely tyres to wheels did not exist in 1846 and the inadequate construction techniques the Company was forced to adopt caused trouble on many engines.

On 25 January 1847, Michael was working an Exeter express up from Swindon with *Queen*. He had just passed Southall station at 50 mph as the down, 4 p.m. Paddington stopping train approached on the opposite line, when he saw a ring of fire, a blur of orange and red sparks, around *Queen*'s off-side driving wheel. As this was the fourth time in nine months he knew what was happening and instantly dodged to the centre of the footplate, his back against the firebox, his head down below its high dome. A second later, as the stopping train passed by, the tyre exploded like shrapnel, great lumps of iron, flung away, forwards and back, stripping off the wheel's brass casing, the boiler handrail and penetrating the carriages of both trains.

In the leading carriage of the stopping train six people occupied one compartment, all friends, including Henry Halt, a butcher from Uxbridge, and his assistant, Henry Bishop, both men sitting with their backs to the engine. They were all returning home in good spirits after attending a court hearing in London where they had been charged with cruelly treating a calf and had been found Not Guilty. Fate apparently disagreed. A piece of iron tyre smashed through the leading end of the carriage, missed the front guard by inches, and sliced down the centre of the vehicle missing all the occupants till it hit the two Henrys, smashing their skulls and butchering their brains. Their bodies were carried off the train and taken to the Red Lion pub just outside the station where they were viewed by members of the Inquest jury, one of whom remarked – in horrified glee – that, while the back of each man's head was entirely missing, their eyes were open and their features peacefully composed – 'except for a slight look of surprise on each face'.

As for Almond, he pulled up as soon as he could, examined his engine for damage and, finding nothing to immobilise it, drove on to Paddington with only his near-side driving wheel making traction on the rail.

Michael Almond's cool judgement coupled with his nerves of steel made him a great favourite with Gooch and won for him the honourable nickname 'Mad Sandy' from railwaymen at large. Gooch showed his high esteem by allocating to him the second of his 'Iron Duke' class 8-ft 'Singles', *Great Britain*, when it came new from Swindon works in July 1847. The engine was Gooch's finest work, the biggest, fastest, best-designed engine in Britain and probably in the world – a suitable machine for Michael 'Mad Sandy' Almond. The gauge controversy was raging in Parliament and in the national newspapers, so *Great Britain* and the other 'Iron Dukes' as they came out of the Works were the 'flagships' of the Great Western Railway, the Company's answer to any criticism of their wide gauge. Speed and haulage trials were made during 1847/8 for the edification of the public as well as to provide information for Swindon drawing office and who better than 'Mad Sandy' to do the driving with a train that included the Gooch dynamometer car and Dan himself riding on the front buffer beam of *Great Britain* at 60 mph and more, taking readings from the instruments fixed to the engine's smokebox. During those trials and on the daily running of the 9.50 a.m. Paddington to Exeter express, speeds of more than 80 mph were reached, velocities not seen on other lines until the 1890s – and bear in mind that, in 1848, brakes were still 'tolerably useless', the signalling no better, so that the railwaymen could justifiably refer to 'Mad Dan' as well as 'Mad Sandy' as the pair went thundering past the lineside policemen on an almost unbraked locomotive, running unprotected into unknown perils at unheard-of speeds.

On 11 May 1848 Michael Almond, with his specially chosen regular mate, Richard Denham, backed *Great Britain* into Paddington to work the 9.15 a.m. Special from Paddington to Didcot – four coaches and a brake van, carrying a party of scientists and engineers, attended by Gooch and other Great Western worthies, for a demonstration of what the 'Iron Duke' class could do on broad-gauge track if they really tried. Obviously Michael had been chosen for the job on account of his reputation – no driver could resist such flattery – and he needed no further hint than to see the eminent gentlemen, with Gooch and the Directors fussing round them, coming up to admire his engine. From the 'Right Away' he threw whatever caution he may have possessed into the cloud of exhaust steam, took his life – and everyone else's – in his hands and let fly. He had to slacken speed through Reading station yard yet covered the 53 miles to a stand at Didcot in 47½ minutes, an average start-to-stop speed of 67 mph.* 'Mad Sandy', having poor brakes braked sooner, lost time slowing down, and therefore would have had to maintain a higher cruising speed especially with the severe slowing through Reading. The privileged passengers came rushing up to congratulate him and Richard – they might have congratulated each other on still being alive.

There were six other 'Iron Dukes' running at that time and their drivers were highly jealous of Michael's feat and the permission he had obviously been given to throw caution to the winds. They had often got down to Didcot in 50 minutes but 47½ – that was a very different matter – and 'Wor Bill' Thompson went so far as to 'pray' that the Directors would give him permission to drive from Paddington to Bristol, 118 miles in *one hour*. He was certain he could do it and asked only that the Company 'look after my people should I have an accident'. The Directors, sadly for railway history, did not take him up on the offer.

The 'Iron Duke' class were too long for existing turntable so larger ones were installed at places where the engines usually reversed – Swindon and Paddington – but one morning, at

---

* This would have been a very reasonable achievement for a 2500 hp diesel in the 1970s when the cruising speed would have been around 80 mph – and when there were very powerful brakes and proper signals.

Didcot, a set of enginemen had to swing an 'Iron Duke' on the table there and had uncoupled the engine from its tender to turn each separately. While the men were pushing and 'pinch-barring' the tender along to the turntable, Michael Almond arrived at the station with a down express. The engine waiting to be turned had its head towards Swindon and as Michael watched it began to move forwards along the siding towards the up main line. The 'Iron Duke' class, in common with all loco-motives of the time, had no brakes at all – their handbrake was on the tender – and the men in charge of this one had omitted to take it out of gear or to open its cylinder steam cocks. Steam, leaking past the regulator valve, entered the cylinders and the engine started away. It pushed through the points and escaped onto the up main, running down it towards Swindon.

Michael shouted to his fireman, Richard Denham, who jumped off and uncoupled *Great Britain* from her train, got back on the engine and the chase was on. He overtook the runaway at Milton, dashed on and arrived at Steventon well ahead of the truant. Here he ordered the astonished policeman to turn his bar on for the up line and to switch the crossover points so as to put the runaway onto the down line. The engine came gliding sedately, low in steam, over the points. Michael let it buffer up gently behind the slowly moving *Great Britain* and then, while his mate put on the handbrake, climbed back over his tender and along the footplating of the truant to put it out of gear and properly close it down. Having done this he shunted it into a siding at Steventon, so that the porters could throw out its fire, and headed back, up the down line, to his train. The passengers had at first been outraged at the apparently wanton disappear-ance of their engine but on being told that the intrepid Almond was away 'saving the day' their mood changed to one of eager anticipation so that Almond and Denham returned to the sound of their passengers' cheering and clapping.

Michael Almond became Foreman at Paddington shed and on 27 June 1873 – his retirement year – he rode on the footplate of *Lord of the Isles* with Driver Groves and Fireman Henderson at the head of the Royal train carrying the Shah of Persia from Paddington to Windsor. This was the year before signal boxes, as we know them, were introduced and all points and signals were still worked by hand by lineside policemen. Alert as ever in his sixty-seventh year, Almond spotted the points set wrong in the Windsor junction at Slough, Driver Groves saw only the disc at 'All Right', and old Michael's timely shout of 'Whoa – the road's wrong' saved the day. The policeman was too overcome with fear at the thought of what might have happened to be of any further assistance so it was Michael Almond who climbed down from the engine and re-set the junction correctly in full view of many bemedalled dignitaries on the train. Alert and decisive to the end he finished his career in a blaze of glory.

While Jim Hurst was known throughout the railway for his quick temper and Michael Almond for his cool nerve and sheer professionalism, Bob Roscoe was regarded with universal affection by railwaymen and the public alike as the most cheerful and warm-hearted of the 'top link' drivers. He was born in Liverpool in 1818 – born, one might say, to be an engine driver – into a family of engineers. All his brothers worked with stationary engines in mills and mines around Lancashire and were credited with various inventions to improve machinery. Bob was twelve years old when the Liverpool & Manchester Railway opened and was immediately attracted to its locomotives – he rode with Jim Hurst and may well have met the Vulcan works apprentice Dan Gooch during those footplate rides. When a driver would not let him ride on the engine, Bob simply stole it, sitting out of sight at the back of the engine's tender – sitting astride a buffer in a demonstration of the greatest possible enthusiasm. He joined the Manchester & Leeds Railway, aged sixteen, in 1834, starting as a cleaner but soon becoming a driver and after ten years joined the Great Western where Gooch gave him the three-year-old *Bright Star* – a 7-ft 'Single', Gooch-designed and Stephenson-built. In April 1847 Gooch's masterwork emerged from Swindon factory – *Iron Duke* – an 8-ft 'Single', at that time the most powerful of engines. Only the most reliable drivers were entrusted with such machines – Jim Hurst does not appear ever to have had one – and Bob Roscoe, a relative newcomer, was issued with *Sultan*, the sixth of the class, when it came new from the works in November 1847. Bob drove *Sultan* on the Paddington to Bristol and the Paddington to Birmingham expresses for twenty years working twelve-hour shifts on a cableless locomotive at speeds of 60 mph through nights of bitter cold or drenching rain with the same unfaltering concentration as through a warm, summer's day. When his eyes were half frozen in the frosty slipstream and his brain craved sleep ceaseless vigilance was essential if he was to keep check of where he was in the darkness so as to know what lay ahead and where to look in order to spot the next little signal lamp as early as possible. The signalling system was primitive, his brakes were quite useless for an emergency stop and his life and those of his passengers depended on his seeing his signals well before he got to them. In this his life was no more difficult than any other 'top link' driver but he was notable, if not unique among express train drivers, for the relaxed and good-humoured manner he adopted towards the rest of humanity in spite of every difficulty.

In those twenty years he had only one black mark against him and that was as a result of using the new, powerful brake with which his train had been fitted. In 1865 the Great Western fitted experimentally to some trains Mr Clarke's patent chain brake by which the driver could operate brake blocks on every wheel in his train. Drivers were very pleased with this and immediately relied on it to bring their trains to a stand at station stops; consequently they approached stations at a faster speed, thus saving much time. However, the Locomotive Department of 1865 did not share their drivers' confidence and several were fined for using the brake; Bob Roscoe was fined £2 in June that year for 'coming into Gloucester station too fast and relying on his brake to stop'. In September 1865, Joseph Armstrong, Locomotive & Carriage Superintendent, issued the following instruction:

Notice to Enginemen

Enginemen must not depend on the continuous breaks [sic] for stopping their trains under ordinary circumstances and the practice of approaching stations and junctions at high speeds and depending on stopping their train by means of these breaks must be entirely discontinued as they are intended to be used only in cases of emergency or when necessary when descending inclines.

Until the Clarke chain brake was withdrawn, about 1870, the fines and the notices continued to be issued; then, for seven or eight years, trains ran with their old – 'tolerably useless' – brakes until the introduction of the first vacuum brake, the 'Sanders', starting with an experimental fitting in 1877.

The occasional fine did not alter the Company's good opinion of a man and in any case, four months later, in January 1866, Bob squared his account. Coming up from Swindon with an express he had the good fortune to see in good time the foxhounds of the Old Berks Hunt standing 'mesmerised' on the track whence they had been led and left by crafty old Reynard – foxes having early on recognised the advantage of railways. Bob was able to stop without running into the pack – a feat meritorious enough to wipe out any amount of illicit use of the chain brake – so he got a half-sovereign from the Master of Hounds and the Great Western, for its part, wrote down the award in big red letters on the line below that recording his fine.

In 1867 Bob was taken off main line expresses, parted from *Sultan* and given Gooch's pride and joy, *Lord of the Isles*, to drive the Windsor trains from Paddington, working a regular day shift so that he would always be fresh to work a Royal train when the need arose. Royal trains were very much part of the GWR London division scene ever since 15 August 1840 when the Dowager Queen Adelaide travelled in the Royal saloon from Wallingford Road to Paddington. The first reigning monarch to use the Great Western had been Frederick IV of Prussia when he went to Windsor for the christening of the Prince of Wales in January 1842 and in June that year Queen

Victoria had travelled on the Great Western for the first time. Since then the Paddington – Windsor route had seen regular traffic in crowned heads, princes and other potentates sometimes on state visits, sometimes as optimistic suitors or merely on a trip out to the theatre and, since an embarrassing incident with a Royal train at Slough in 1846, the Great Western had been at pains to appoint only the best men to the work. In June 1846 the engine of a Royal train failed and all that was readily available to work the train to Paddington was a 2–4–0 goods engine with 5-ft diameter wheels called *Buffalo* driven by John Harle. John was twenty-six years, had been a driver for barely two years, the Directors were concerned and Charles Saunders, the Company's eminent secretary, gave him strict instructions not to show off – the 18 miles to Paddington were not to be covered in less than 30 minutes and preferably a bit longer, time was of no great importance, giving Victoria a smooth ride was – furthermore *Buffalo* was not suitable for high speed and one failure on a Royal train was sufficient. But John was unable to restrain the feelings of pride that welled up within him. *Buffalo* set off like an antelope, giving the Sovereign a very rough ride and completing the run in 25 minutes with a top speed near 60 mph. Her Majesty had been alarmed and John had a sovereign docked from his wages for disobedience to the Directors' orders.

Bob Roscoe had the experience and personality to be entrusted with monarchs and – of at least as great importance – with the person of Sir Daniel Gooch. The 9.5 a.m. broad-gauge train from Windsor to Paddington was the train on which he used to travel to work each day and whatever else was re-timed in the time books, whatever else was reduced to narrow gauge, this train remained unaltered from 1867 until the abolition of the broad gauge on the branch in June 1883 – and Bob was its driver. So regular was he on this trip that, notwithstanding the fact that Gooch also used it every day, the 9.5 Windsor was known as 'Roscoe's train'. In 1878 there were only two 'through' broad-gauge trains in each direction between Windsor and Paddington including the 6.15 a.m. Paddington and its return working 'Roscoe's train'. There were also three broad-gauge coaches slipped off of down expresses at Slough which were then worked to and from Windsor in narrow-gauge trains, the broad-gauge carriages jutting out sideways beyond the rest by about 3 ft. To couple the apparently incompatible, 'dummy carriages' were used, equipped with huge, elongated buffers and laterally sliding drawgear. It was normal on mixed-gauge lines for the working timetable to indicate which trains were broad and which were narrow gauge but on the Windsor branch matters were haphazard, broad-gauge carriages ran promiscuously in narrow-gauge trains and the best that could be managed by way of written warning to staff was a vague, singular announcement: 'The gauge of trains is uncertain.'

Occasionally the uncertainty caught someone unawares. On 19 August 1878 the considerably accident-prone Bill Chives had worked a narrow-gauge train from Paddington to Windsor and had taken his engine back to Slough to turn it before parking in a siding for a bite to eat. Unbeknown to him one of his engine's buffers was ever so slightly foul of the branch line's broad-gauge rail; a narrow-gauge train rolled in from Windsor hauling a broad-gauge carriage at the rear; and the 'dummy carriage' came into no uncertain contact with Chives' engine, removing its buffer and splintering a great deal of wood. Bill went before the Board in considerable trepidation but they took a miraculously lenient view and let him off with a 'Caution'.

Bob worked the Windsor branch blamelessly with *Lord of the Isles* until 1883 when the line was reduced to narrow gauge only and he retired from the line after forty years' service. In his twenty-one years on the branch he became an Institution, admired for his geniality and good grace as much as for his skill as a driver. For every Royal train he drove he earned an extra sovereign and many a Sovereign he drove, for it was not only Queen Victoria who used his trains – proud Tsar, haughty Archduchess or silky Shah all went up to see the Queen-Empress in the safe keeping of white-corduroyed Bob Roscoe.

SEVEN

Brunel's Blind Spot

The Great Western drew its recruits from a vast well of men – the energetic, the enterprising, the slow countryman, the eccentric and ingenious – gave them all a job for life and took upon itself the remarkable amalgamation of all their characters. Train guards were, in the early years, chosen for their stature – all were over 5 ft 10 in. tall – and for their bearing; footmen or butlers were eagerly taken into the service for their elegant manners which were so useful when dealing with the Great Western's wealthy or aristocratic clientele.

Ben Jeans was valet to Lord Carlisle who begged him not to risk his life in such a dangerous business as railways but Ben left him to seek his fortune on the Great Western in 1842 and brought to the service of the Company the erect and dignified deportment, scrupulously correct speech of a Court Chamberlain. Like the porters, Ben wore not a uniform but a livery. His top hat was held on by leather side-stays but unlike a porter's topper, his was covered in the finest beaverskin. He also wore a heavy top coat, a frock coat and waistcoat all in dark green with brass buttons and white trousers – the imposing effect of this then being marred by his being obliged to sit in open carriages and get drenched with the 2nd class passengers; even in the mid-1850s guards travelled in open vans though there was a tarpaulin to cover passengers' luggage.

Ben Jeans became the regular guard of a Paddington to Birkenhead train in 1854, working right through in each direction and sleeping each night alternately in London and Birkenhead. Throughout the terribly cold winter of 1854/5 – the

'Crimean Winter' – he rode often as not in an open van and whatever harmful effect such weather had on the passengers, now in completely enclosed but unheated carriages, hugging rapidly cooling tins of hot water, Ben came to no harm. He stuck to the job with commendable imperturbability, remained solely on that duty for forty-two years and became an institution – the train being known from end to end of the line as 'Jeans' train'. As a man of over seventy he still made his professional flourish, leaping into his van as the train steamed away at 7 mph and he retired after four million miles and fifty-four years' service, 'mourned' by bankers, aristocrats and politicians, his retirement present from these worthies being subscribed to by another man destined to become an institution: W. E. Gladstone.

The Great Western provided a wonderful opportunity for a stable life, a life of some responsibility, status and regular pay to thousands of men who would otherwise never have known such things. Henry Bircham left his home at East Bergholt, near Ipswich, in 1842 and tramped down to the docks where he found a captain willing to take him aboard his sailing coaster and let him work his passage to London. A few days later Henry was disembarked on a London quayside, alone, without a single friend, his possessions in a bundle held in one hand. He was twelve years old. Sleeping rough at first, then over the bakery where he found work, he gradually moved up the many-runged ladder of status till he entered gentleman's service, eventually arriving in the London household of the Marquess of Landsdowne. But though he was well placed he was not secure, the household moved with the seasons, he was not always needed so, in 1854, he joined the Great Western as a guard and worked till he was seventy-two – a tall, dignified man with a calm face over a high, sharp-edged, stiff collar, wearing also a perfectly folded silk cravat, a waistcoat draped with a gold watch chain to his guard's gold watch, jacket, frock coat with carnation in the buttonhole, brass buttons and all topped off by a pill-box hat braided, in gold, GUARD. He looked it, every inch.

Steady as well-trained soldiers, the guards were the

embodiment of the aristocratic Great Western, the Company's ambassadors, ready to deal with any emergency. In Victorian times it seems that cutting one's throat and/or jugular vein was – if not a craze – than at least a favourite, fashionably melodramatic way of doing away with oneself and those unfortunates who chose this form of exit were not fussy as to where they made it – as Harry Northcott of an Oxford to Paddington express discovered when he found just such a gushing passenger. The man had severed his throat and jugular with the aptly named 'cut-throat' razor. Northcott simply held the man together with both hands until the train reached Didcot where he shouted for help. Mr Doyne, Senior Surgeon at the Oxford Eye Hospital, was elsewhere on the train and came rushing up in response to the call. He sutured the man's ghastly wounds while the unflappable Northcott kept the blood vessels pinched tight between his fingers till the doctor was able to attend to them.

In the security of long service, men grew into the parts required of them – the dignified guard or the old gaffer of the track, gnarled and weatherbeaten as an ancient apple tree. Henry Gardener was born in the village of Far Oakridge, remote in the beech woods high above Chalford in the Gloucestershire 'Golden Valley'. In 1846, when he was nineteen, he left the farmwork which had toughened his muscles to whipcord and joined the gangs of George Bennett, the contractor to the Great Western for the maintenance of the then newly opened railway through Sapperton tunnel from Kemble to Gloucester. Henry Gardener's gang was responsible for four miles of line from Chalford up the steep incline to the head of the beautiful and precipitous valley, down through the tunnel to the sidings in the quarry-like excavation at the Kemble end. Every day he walked to work from Oakridge, down the steep valley side, over the locks of the Thames & Severn canal, up the cliff-like steepness to Frampton Mansell where he met the railway line and walked down to Chalford to sign on for the seven o'clock start. Having done that he and his mates shouldered their heavy tools and walked to the site of their day's work to shovel and dig for twelve hours before tackling the long walk home through that deep valley. Only once did he rise to public notice, when an excursion train going up the hill broke a coupling chain and while the guard wrestled with his handbrake to bring the carriages to a stand, Henry, remembering that another train was due to follow the excursion, raced down to Chalford and stopped it. For fifty-six years, until he was seventy-four and had been ganger of the length for forty-four years, that four miles of track was his world – that, the walk through the beeches summer and winter and his cottage with its garden in Far Oakridge.

The perils to which passengers were subjected as the result of a lack of proper brakes, proper wheels or proper signalling caused Brunel to suggest on 14 January 1847 that a man be employed to sit on the back of each passenger engine's tender and 'keep a steady, vigilant look-out along the train so that if sufficient cause may come to his observation he may at once communicate with the enginemen and stop the train'. Gooch modified four tenders to start with, putting on the off-side of each a hooded, iron seat which looked a bit like an up-ended coracle and placed a walk-way from side to side over the buffers so that the man could inspect the near-side of the train. At stations, it was suggested, the man could examine and grease axle boxes and/or help with passengers' luggage. These arrangements were brought into use on 14 October 1847 – the uniquely Great Western 'travelling porter' had arrived. There was not a more dangerous job on the railway. At 50–60 mph the tender shook and jolted along, jarring the seated porter, threatening to throw him under the wheels as he moved across the narrow walk-way to peer along the near-side of the train. It seems an outrageous remedy yet Brunel was not an outrageous man and indeed, there were plenty of intrepid individuals willing to take the job on at 25 shillings a week.

One day the travelling porter on a train saw a leather strap dangling loose from luggage on the near-side of a 1st class carriage and stepped across from tender to train intent on re-fastening the buckle. The strap was banging against the side of the coach and was probably making a great nuisance for the occupants – there might be a shilling in it for the porter if he put the job right. He reached the strap just as the train ran onto Maidenhead bridge and at that moment someone opened the compartment door with such force as to sweep the porter off his perch on the footboard; he fell against the parapet of the bridge and was killed instantly.

In winter the travelling porter sat in sub-zero slipstreams, frozen numb and quite unable to move to carry out his duties, indeed, it is a recorded fact that on occasions the poor man would be quite unable to leave his seat at stations because not only was he frozen rigid into a sitting position but his clothing had frosted to the icy metal. Then he had to be, literally, cut free of the seat and carried to the refreshment room fire to be thawed out with brandy. The iron seat was quickly dubbed the 'Iron Coffin' by the men but it continued in use until 1864 when some genius thought of threading a cord through eye-hole brasses fixed along the eaves of the carriages to connect with a brass gong on the engine's tender or to the engine's whistle so that a passenger in trouble could give warning to the train crew to stop. While one cannot help but wonder why Brunel did not think of this in the first place, the longevity of the 'Iron Coffin' was due in large part to the conservatism of the Great Western Directors who fought hard against the introduction of the 'communication cord' on the grounds that it would allow the passengers to interfere with the running of the train.

Brunel seemed to have a blind spot where safety was concerned, the minutiae of civil engineering being one thing, the details of operating a railway being quite a different matter, with the notable exception of inventing the brake whistle. When he developed his signalling system for the GWR he ignored the electric telegraph which was there for him to use and which would have enabled a certain minimum *distance* to be kept between trains and instead left his policemen working 'blind' and keeping only a minimum time between trains which guaranteed nothing. His signals were tall and large enough to be seen from a great way off but in fog they were useless and, as they used a white light by night to indicate 'All Right', could be and were confused with candles in houses or street lights with fatal results.

He arranged for a disc of sheet metal of 4 ft diameter and perforated to lessen wind resistance, to be placed directly over and at right angles to a cross bar 8 ft by 1 ft, also perforated; both were painted bright red and mounted as one fixture on a wooden mast 30–60 ft tall. By turning the mast through 90° the policeman could bring one or other shape to face oncoming traffic. The system was soon refined. The clumsy mast, heavy to swivel, was made a fixture and supported by guy wires while an iron spindle to carry the signal rose up through ring bolts screwed into the mast – thus the policeman's lot was lighter and the signal, better supported, was much less likely to be blown down in a strong wind. Lamps for night signalling – red for 'Danger' and white for 'All Right' – had once been hoisted up the mast as required but the improved signals had a lamp fixed to the spindle with swivelling innards so that the aspect changed as the signal turned. Beside the disc and crossbar signals stood the 'Caution' board with a green and a red face. At night the board was replaced by a lamp on a short post, the lamp being a square box with a clear glass front into which could be placed a blank shutter, a red or a green slide.

If the train which had passed was a goods train the 'Danger' signal was kept on for eight minutes and the 'Caution' was shown for a further seven minutes*.

The policeman or switchman sheltered in a door-less sentry box, 3 ft square and mounted on a pivot so that it could be turned out of the wind but even so, on a raw, autumn night or freezing February day it must have been a mind-numbing job. His sentry hut, called a 'box' from the outset, often stood on a cobbled area close to one of his sets of signals and from his box he walked his 'beat', altering the points, swivelling his signals

---

* 1842–52, all trains equal, signals 3 min. 'Danger', 7 min. 'Caution'; 1852–end, passenger trains' rear protected by 5 min. 'Danger', 5 min. 'Caution'.

and changing the coloured shades in his glass – all as the minutes passed after a train had gone by. Two men worked each box, twelve hours a day for six days and while one man took Sunday off the other man worked eighteen or twenty-four hours to cover him. The box became their home and many men cultivated the lineside bank to make up, perhaps, for not having time to look after their garden at home, although it would not surprise me to discover that some men had the energy, after a twelve-hour shift and a walk home, to dig their own garden as well. They must have been the toughest of men, working without any electrical or mechanical safeguards to assist their natural vigilance and thus keep trains out of trouble yet the Company doctor would direct a man to be a policeman having turned him down as of insufficient physique to be a porter! Tough men they were; the Great Western offered an annual bonus of £5 (weekly wages 20–22 shillings) to any policeman who could work for a year without making a mistake. The bonus was paid in six-monthly instalments and Company records show that most men collected.

But even the fittest had to have a pee and on occasions, due to the weakness of the signalling system, this resulted in terrifying disasters. Switchman Constable Pargetter was on duty at Shrivenham station on 10 May 1848 with a beat that covered the entire station layout from the sidings and goods shed at the west end to the level crossing 100 yds east of the little, flint and stone station building. He had two disc-and-crossbar signals to work, the down line signal was on the level crossing while the up line signal was 50 yds from the crossing, towards the station. Great Western express trains were then at the peak of their fame, running at speeds of 60 mph, and Daniel Gooch had toured the line to ensure that all signals were visible at a good distance, re-siting those that were not. Shrivenham's up signal could be seen from Acorn bridge over the road and canal 1½ miles to the west.

At 3 p.m. Pargetter closed the level-crossing gates against the lane in readiness for the noon express from Exeter due past

Shrivenham at about 3.3 p.m. He had a clear view along the tracks, east and west, all was clear and in order, his discs were turned on, his 'Caution' board turned edgeways so as to be practically invisible to drivers. He leant back against the gate to wait. Without any electric telegraph to advise him he was unaware that the Exeter was running late – its connection off the South Devon Railway from Plymouth had arrived late at Exeter, two extra coaches had been added at Bristol and as a result the 'Firefly' class engine had got into trouble on the uphill section through Box tunnel, her 7-ft diameter driving wheels slipping round on the rails without traction and thus losing more time.

At 3.5 p.m. Porter Weybury emerged contentedly from the Victoria tavern, close to the crossing; he wiped the last of his lunchtime beer from his moustache, waved to the top-hatted policeman and strolled away to the station. A horse and cart coming slowly along the lane from Shrivenham turned in through the station gates – Kent's cart from Highworth, noted Pargetter. The policeman waited with growing impatience for the express, a farmer in his gig had arrived at the gates from Ashbury but Pargetter dared not let him cross the line and when, at 3.17, the down stopping train arrived, he hurriedly turned the bar on behind it and rushed across to the Victoria – not for a beer but to have a pee.

At the station Mr Corbett Hudson, the Station Clerk, waved the stopping train on its way and returned to the booking office to sell tickets for the 'Parliamentary' train due down in another twenty minutes while Weybury and his assistant Willoughby went into the goods shed to load Kent's cart with some of the contents of a coal wagon. Willoughby was a local jack of all trades who for three months had stood in for the regular porter, Copley, who was supposedly ill but who had found some other work and rented his railway job out to Willoughby. Copley, being then considerably in funds, spent his percentage of Willoughby's wages in support of the Victoria tavern.

To bring the coal truck down for unloading, the porters and

Kent's carter had first to push a horse-box and cattle truck out
of the goods shed towards the station along the siding which
joined the main line at the foot of the platform ramp. Sidings
then had no 'throw-off' or 'trap' point to protect the main line so
without giving the matter any thought the men shoved the two
wagons onto the up main line; the cattle truck was nearest the
station, standing right on the main line end of the points, and
the horse-box was just 'foul' of the main line though still on the
siding. If Pargetter had not been otherwise engaged he could
not have failed to have seen what the men had done – but he was
not there and his up disc remained on.

Bob Roscoe had backed his *Sultan* onto the Exeter express at
Swindon as soon as the 'Firefly' class engine had gone away to
shed and he took the train away twenty-three minutes late.
Sultan was one of Gooch's magnificent 'Iron Duke' class 'single
wheelers' with 8-ft-diameter driving wheels; it was just six
months old and Bob had driven it since it came fresh from
Swindon works. His instructions were that he was not to make
up any time so he let *Sultan* cross Acorn bridge at 55 mph with
Shrivenham's up signal showing as a tiny red dot over the
parapet of Bourton bridge spanning the cutting ahead. Bob had
the road and let her run. *Sultan* shot under the bridge at the west
end of Shrivenham station in all her brassy, broad-gauge, glory.
Bob saw the situation 150 yds ahead just as Weybury saw him
and came running forward, arms outstretched. Bob made the
brake whistle boom to alert the guard so he would apply his
brake and keep the couplings stretched tight but did not brake
his engine and struck home hard, relying on his superior velocity
to smash through the obstruction. *Sultan* ripped into the side of
the cattle truck and brushed past it, the wrecked wagon tearing
open the leading 2nd class carriage. The horse-box was struck
nearly end-on and seemed to explode. Its wheels flew through
the air, axles bent double, to land in the booking office doorway
just as Corbett Hudson was coming out. He was hurt but by
some miracle was not killed. Horrible splinters of wood flew like
spears and the truck roof, coming off clean like a lid, took off

Sultan's chimney and only just missed decapitating Roscoe and his mate before falling on the tender.

Four people were spilled out onto the track and killed, fourteen were badly injured and the station staff had to forcibly restrain a looter who was in the process of removing a gold watch and chain from the corpse of a clergyman. The dead were lodged in the stable at the Victoria and several of the injured remained in the tavern, seriously ill, where – to quote the Foreman of the Inquest jury – they were 'nightly serenaded by the raucous company of the Tap Room' led by the three-months' sick Porter Copley.

Wagons appearing on the main line in front of trains were a common hazard so long as the Company refused to spend money on catch points but instead used a small, cast-iron block clamped over one rail where the catch point ought to have been. Three wagons were shunted into a siding at Wallingford Road station during March 1865, their brakes not pinned down properly, if at all. A mad, March gale sprang up and blew them along the siding with such force that they jumped the little block, pushed through the hand-lever-operated point at the main line end and were promptly pounced upon and splintered into matchwood by a passing goods train – entirely to the astonishment of the on-duty policeman George Danford. When a man was thought to have committed an offence he was summoned to appear before a committee of the Board in the magnificence of the Boardroom at Paddington. Behind the seated gentlemen there hung, from 1855, a full-length portrait of Charles Russell, eminent Chairman of the Company from 1839 to 1855, so that the wretched offender could either face the flesh-and-blood gaze of the committee or raise his eyes to meet the elegant, slightly mocking, slightly disdainful stare of the retired Chairman. Such a summons was, from 1855, known as 'Going to see the Picture'. George Danford duly received his unrefusable invitation and waited with the greatest apprehension upon the Board. Luckily the gentlemen were in a reasonable mood, George was able to convince them that he was not to blame, and returned to Wallingford Road in an equivalent state of euphoria, his wages intact.

Tiredness was the greatest enemy of railwaymen – and the travelling public – when life depended on the alertness of each man's mind yet thousands of men spent their night shifts craving sleep. Very early one morning in 1850 while it was still quite dark, John Clark, the policeman working the East box beat at Swindon, saw a white light appear far up the line towards Didcot. He thought it was time for the down 'Limited Mail' so he rang his handbell, checked his road and turned on his white light. On the station the porters hurried about, pulling barrow-loads of mail into position for this, the most important train of the day, the only one that did not wait the full ten minutes at Swindon, the only train where even the Directors of the Company had to book in advance for a seat in the single passenger coach. The station staff got everything ready, one, very privileged passenger was standing, waiting but no train arrived, so Mr Pell, the Station Inspector, walked out to East box to see what had happened.

'Where's the Mail then, John?'

The policeman pointed eastwards. 'There – see its headlamp? I think it must be stopped up there, perhaps we ought to send the pilot out.'

Mr Pell looked hard for several seconds and then said, half laughing, half in disgust, 'That's not a headlamp – that's a very bright star, low down.'

At Reading station in 1850 the Police Inspector was Mr Bath and among his switchmen/constables was a Mr Belcher. Mr Bath was going his rounds late one night and came upon Belcher in his box with his eyes shut.

'Aha!' cried Bath triumphantly, 'caught you asleep, Belcher.'

'I was not asleep,' retorted the constable, his bonus before his eyes.

'You had your eyes shut – you were asleep.'

'Well, so would you have your eyes shut if you had to sit out here in this cold – I've got to keep them warm somehow.'

Constable Belcher survived to become Station Master at Wool-
hampton.

Inspectors like Mr Bath were not popular with the men if
they did too much midnight prowling and more than one zealot
had his ardour cooled by a good, hard rap on the head from a
policeman's truncheon, the wily constable apologising profusely
afterwards, saying that he had unfortunately mistaken the
Inspector for a gang of telegraph-wire thieves.

On another night at Reading about 1850 porters Ben Angell
and John Dawes were pushing a horse-box from a siding into
the platform of the down station, a move requiring them to first
push it out onto the down main line before the switchman could
turn the points from main to platform line. The policeman did
this for them and then went away to deal with another shunt,
forgot all about the horse-box move and a few minutes later
turned his disc on for a down train to pass. With the points still
set for the last move the train swerved into the platform line and
smashed into the horse-box, and a buffer, flying through the air,
killed Ben Angell. He was twenty-two with a wife and small
daughter.

Reading station was one of several laid out on the Brunellian,
'one-sided', principle whereby up trains and down trains called
at separate, self-contained stations which stood along loops off
the main lines and which were ranged along the south side only
– the side nearest to the town. Brunel hoped that this would be
more convenient to the passengers because there was no footbridge or subway stairs for them to negotiate with heavy luggage
but passengers changing trains had to trek 100 yds, unsheltered,
from one station to the other – which was very unpopular. The
station was tolerably nightmarish to operate because up trains
calling there had to cross and then re-cross the down main line,
extra tracks were added piecemeal, there was no real warning of
the approach of any train and no interlocking between points
and signals throughout the chaotically scrambled layout. The
station was divided into three beats – East box, Middle box and
West box and a disc and crossbar stood at 'Danger' at each end

of the layout and on the Newbury branch in reversal of the usual practice out of deference to the complications and inherent dangers of the place. Drivers were instructed to approach the station with caution at all times and that was about the scope of the safety regulations for the place. The switchmen each looked after their own patch, allowing shunting movements to take place within and outside their 'home' signals until they thought a train was due – or it blew its whistle at them – then they had to clear the line quickly, set their points and turn their discs on. This indicated to the driver that some route, known only to the switchmen, was cleared; the disc-and-crossbar signal gave no indication of which route was set; and on at least one occasion a dog-tired policeman forgot to turn a set of points and sent the 'Flying Dutchman' through the platform loop instead of down the main line. Luckily the loop was not occupied, the driver had already taken the usual precaution of slowing down for Reading and the stability of the broad gauge did the rest as the world's fastest train swung sharply into the loop and back out onto the main line at the far end while the policeman clung to the handle of the facing point capstan – in a dead faint.

Ideally the Reading policemen should have got ready five minutes before the arrival of a train. If a down train was due the East box man checked his points and tracks and then gave a hearty peal on his bell which hung on a framework near his box. The Middle box man, hearing this, repeated the warning peal to the West box man; these two checked that everything was in order, then the West box man held up a white flag to the Middle and the Middle box man repeated this to the West box man who then turned his disc on. How they knew which route was required by the approaching train is not certain – neither is it at all clear how each man reached the same conclusion. It was an incredibly hit-or-miss affair depending for its success on the men knowing the timetable by heart – and on the trains arriving in their proper sequence.

The electric telegraph began to be used, between Ealing and Paddington, from October 1861 to alert Paddington to the approach of a train; in November the system had been extended to work to and from Twyford so, possibly, it was further extended to cover Reading and beyond. The method was there to advise station masters – not switchmen – and any information the telegraph clerk managed to communicate to the distant switchmen was entirely a matter of luck. By 1864 rail traffic on the Great Western had increased greatly compared with 1844 yet the 1844 signalling system for double track lines was still, with very minor improvements, in use. Any semblance of safety depended on the policeman and driver maintaining the sharpest possible look-out – especially in the pitch-dark night – and even then their vigilance had to be supplemented with a very large slice of luck.

On 15 January 1864 at Pangbourne, in the depths of that winter night, with the clammy damp rising off the Thames, a goods train stopped by the water crane and the enginemen prepared to take on water. Policeman James Attwood, the switchman, turned his bar and red light on and went to the driver to ask him to shunt his train through the crossover to the down main so as to clear the up line for the express from Birmingham. The driver finished filling his tender at the water crane while Attwood walked to the crossover and set both ends right for the move. Just as the train was half-way over, Mr Glasson, the Station Master, arrived on the scene having been absent from the station on some errand. He immediately ordered the goods driver to bring his train back to the up main so that it would not delay the 'Limited Mail' due on the down line. He also ordered Sam Oakley, the guard of the goods train, to walk back a mile, showing a red light and at the mile point behind his train to put down three detonators and to stand over them with his red light so that the driver of the next up train would have plenty of warning to pull up.

All good stuff. The 'Limited Mail' was more important than the Birmingham and proper protection had been ordered between the latter and the goods train. Unfortunately for the plan, Sam did not go back far enough, especially as the line curved steadily in a very deep, narrow cutting making a distant sighting of his signal impossible. The Birmingham came up at 50 mph, had insufficient warning to stop and crashed into the rear of the stationary goods train, tumbling wagons left and right, blocking both lines but injuring no one. The noise of the collision was heard at Pangbourne and Mr Glasson immediately sent 'Line Blocked' to Reading and Goring telegraph offices on his single-needle telegraph instrument. Mr Bland, on duty at the Reading office, dashed out onto the platform and was able to warn the driver of the 'Limited Mail' so that he went away with a 'Caution' for Pangbourne. The regulations did not require him to stay at Reading till 'Line Clear' was received so he went on his way without actually knowing what was blocking the line. When the wreckage had been sufficiently cleared to allow single-line working trains began to pass between Goring and Reading using the down line only. No train could enter on the single-track section unless the solitary man appointed as pilot-man was either riding on the engine or had personally ordered the driver to proceed – thus only one train at a time could occupy the single track and head-on collisions were avoided. The pilotman opened up the single line correctly, going down the down line on the engine of a train and handing out written notification of the state of affairs to the station masters at Pangbourne and Goring who would then inform their own men. (Tilehurst station did not exist.) The telegraph clerk at Reading was the co-ordinator of the arrangements and as telegraph operator as well was in a hectic position. It was his job to inform the Police Inspector at Reading, Mr Hales, of what was taking place in the deep, bitter, darkness. He failed to do so.

At Goring an express from Bristol was waiting; the pilotman got off the down train, climbed aboard the up train's footplate and ordered it away up the down line to Reading. Now, this was a broad-gauge train but since 1861 a third rail had been added between Oxford and Paddington to allow the narrow gauge (as the Great Western called it) or standard gauge (as everyone else called it) to run from north to south coasts and from Worcester to Paddington. As a result of this mixed gauge all points had three movable blades instead of two and the switchmen had the additional mental burden of moving the correct blades according to the gauge of the approaching train. This was of little moment at a place such as Pangbourne but at big junctions such as Reading it was of crucial importance and added enormously to the intricacies and worries of a switchman's life. The up Bristol express approached its Reading call sedately, which was just as well. Switchman Collins had, a few minutes before, turned the narrow-gauge blades of a point in the down main to allow a shunt to take place; the broad-gauge blade, not being required, he left set for straight running and, having seen to this job, he went off somewhere, leaving the work to Inspector Hales. Set like this the points in the down main were a trap for any broad-gauge train approaching them *up* the down line. An almost impossible event yet it was gradually happening due to a remarkable succession of oversights. Mr Hales stood among the maze of tracks, literally in the dark about several important facts, and watched the approach of the up train, impassively at first, then with curiosity as it seemed to be rather far over to the left, then with astonishment when he realised it was running on what ought to have been the down line. He had prepared the road for the up line – how far would it run before coming to grief on some unprepared point? He watched helplessly as it trundled past, his heart in his mouth. Was he about to see his job crash about his ears? A few seconds later the engine ran off the rails at Collins' trap and amid the sound of rending wood and bending metal, it ploughed to a stand on *Olde England*. Up before 'The Picture', at Paddington, the sentences were handed out. Collins, Hales and Bland had long and blameless careers behind them and this large credit balance saved them from more than a verbal reprimand. Mr Glasson got a rap over the knuckles – even though he had left his station without permission which usually carried a penalty of a fine at least. It was down to Sam Oakley, lowliest of them all, to carry the can for the entire affair. He was dismissed for negligence.

In March 1874 signal boxes as we know them were brought into use on the entire route from Paddington to Bristol working a mixture of disc-and-crossbar and semaphore signals. Each box had a row of point and signal levers interlocked by a clever mechanism to prevent the wrong one being pulled and electric bells and indicators enabled each signalman to communicate with the man on each side of him up and down the line so that trains could be signalled along the line in a routine of bell codes. Rules and regulations governed all actions of the men where trains were concerned, movements were strictly controlled and the design was to keep a proper distance from the train ahead. Each signal box was a proper, roofed and glazed shelter for the signalman, furnished with a fire and oven, a chair and a locker for his gear and into these havens of comfort, out of the weather, went the tough old policemen, still in their lineside uniform of top hat and frock coat.

The antique and chaotic layout at Reading had only worked at all in the past by allowing the East, Middle and West switchmen complete discretion in the movement of trains. When it became controlled by the same men working the East, Middle and West signal boxes, using modern, interlocked, signalling and strict safety rules it just came to a grinding halt with trains queuing for miles in each direction. The Superintendent of the Line, George Nugent Tyrrell, was displeased and told the Reading men: 'This will not do – the public are impatient of delay.' Which was all very well but the men were only applying the rules and the system he had helped to devise. In spite of the new-found comfort of their signal boxes the horny old switch-men sighed for the good old days as they battled with levers that would unlock only if they pulled in the correct sequence or would not unlock at all if a pair of points was set wrong. One old sweat is recorded as saying, 'It's like trying to run with your legs tied together. You can't do a thing for "clearing points" and locking. What's the use of a signal that you can't take off? That's what I'd like to know.'

EIGHT

Dangerous Procedures

One fine day in 1865 a blind man, led only by his stick, groped his way into the booking hall of Usk station, found the booking window and tapped on the glass partition. The wooden shutter behind the glass was raised by the Station Master. 'Yes please?' he asked.

'A ticket to Monmouth,' replied the blind man rather too sharply for the Station Master's liking.

'Eighteen pence,' he retorted in like manner.

The blind man thrust a piece of grimy paper through the aperture in the partition, saying, in a kind of Welsh accent, 'I am in the service of the Lord.'

'Which don't entitle you to free tickets,' replied the Station Master as he unfolded the paper. It was a request for money, purporting to come from some conveniently remote, Merioneth-shire valley, to enable the God-fearing inhabitants to purchase a harmonium for their chapel.

The Station Master dropped the shutter and walked round to the blind beggarman in the hallway. He reeked of the local tavern, smelling as if he had spent enough donations on spirits and tobacco to have brought a Willis organ for the valley dwellers. 'Come along now, you'll be safer in the office.' He took the man's arm and steered him into the room as his clerk wrinkled up his nose and glared. 'Look after him till I get back,' ordered the Station Master.

'Where's he gone now, then?' asked the inebriated beggar anxiously.

'To get the police, I shouldn't wonder,' snapped the clerk. At this the prisoner broke into song, a hymn, out of tune and very loud. He could not have been Welsh, as all Welshmen sing like angels when they are drunk, but the subtlety of such proof of the man's blackguardism was lost on the clerk, who required no proof and cared not a jot for the man's nationality. The hymn was long and painful, shouts of protest had no effect and at the end of the sixth verse, with the seventh hanging over him like a physical threat, the clerk admitted defeat and went outside to await his colleague's return.

As soon as he had gone the blind man made his escape onto the platform but fell over the edge onto the rails where he lay, his leg broken, bellowing for help in the accents of Brislington. The Station Master had indeed gone for constabulary assistance and arrived with a stout policeman. Between them they lifted the wretched man onto the platform where he lay in great pain until a horse and cart arrived to take him to the Workhouse Infirmary. Usk station settled down in peace until the next time.

Stations were important focal-points in the nineteenth century and attracted every sort of person. Faringdon Road station, later named Challow, appeared to be just a lonely, wayside halt, remote in the Berkshire vale but it was in fact of the greatest importance to the town of Faringdon seven miles away and also to a wide scattering of villages, so much so that, in 1862, 35,000 people trod its wooden platforms. The Station Master, especially in a small place, was a man of status like the parson or the doctor and usually kept a servant or two; his Company-built house usually being provided with a system of bell-pulls in each room connected by wires to a row of variously sized bells on the kitchen wall by which means the maid could be summoned. If a Station Master stayed for long enough he would become an institution in his own right. At Steventon the Beck family were 'hereditary' Station Masters, the post being held, father to son to grandson for eighty years.

Almost everything that required to be moved went by rail. Nineteenth-century roads were so bad, especially in the countryside, that it was quicker and cheaper to send goods by circuitous rail routes than by the apparently shorter road route.* When Faringdon railway station was being built, the stone for it came from William Bartlett's yard in Witney by rail through Oxford and Didcot – thirty-five miles instead of thirteen by road. Racehorses, foxhounds to the Meet, furniture, farmers with their pigs to the fair, produce and luggage-laden passengers were driven, portered, barrowed and loaded, across platforms too narrow to accommodate the traffic, too short to allow all the carriages of a train to stand alongside. The forecourts of even small country stations were busy with traffic: local traders' carts, the 'Fly' carriage ferrying passengers to and from the best hotel of the area, a poor girl selling flowers, itinerant boys hoping for a halfpenny for carrying a bag or holding a horse. All the large stations had their supernumeraries including mere loungers and pickpockets. For years Reading station suffered a plague of skilful thieves until the arrival of Inspector May who could spot the most anonymous pickpocket, stalk him and nail him in the very act of pinching a purse or nipping off with a watch.

The Great Western almost went bankrupt in 1865 – Dan Gooch was away laying the first transatlantic cable and came back just in time to straighten out the Company by the use of the most stringent economy – so that for years afterwards the Directors were very loth to spend money on anything. By the mid-1870s the Great Western was in a chaotic state as traffic increased in leaps and bounds but investment in new equipment did not. Passengers wrote complaining letters to the Directors –

* *Rates Book Headings and Instructions, 1890*

Pianos by passenger train; Phonographs on wheels; Biers on four wheels; Bicycles with two wheels but three or four saddles to be charged 50% less; Works of art lent by South Kensington Museum to go at special rates; Gentlemen and their hunters to the Meet; Returned empty pork pie hampers to Melton Mowbray; Troupes of Equestrian Entertainers, reduced rates for, and also Music Hall artistes travelling with their baggage; All dogs to be properly muzzled before travelling by train – the GER will not accept dogs with pieces of cloth or wire tied around their snouts.

often comparing the Great Western most unfavourably with the London & South Western – and the Directors complained to the Superintendent of the Line about the 'lack of energy of our porters' or the 'lack of punctuality of our trains'. I get the impression that there was no love lost between Tyrrell and the Board, whose Chairman was the ex-Locomotive Superintendent, as he took every opportunity to shift the blame off his Traffic Department men onto Gooch's engines or onto the Board as a whole. On 14 September 1876 the timekeeping of the 5.30 a.m. Paddington to Plymouth broad-gauge train was discussed at a meeting of Divisional Superintendents – the Directors, having had some rather cutting letters from the public, wanted to know why it ran continuously late. Mr Tyrrell stated, for the record, that 'broad-gauge engines do not pull away as fast as narrow-gauge engines' and went on to say that owing to a shortage of carriages he was unable to maintain each train as a 'set' unlike the much-praised L&SWR whose trains were marshalled in a constant 'set-order' so that the more numerous L&SWR porters could place their barrows at just the right part of the platform to load luggage or mail directly into the van when the train stopped and marshal the passengers so they were 'right' in front of the carriages of their class – furthermore, he added darkly, 'the 5.30 a.m. Paddington was formerly 1st and 2nd class only but since the Directors have thrown it open to 3rd class its character is very much altered and great difficulty is experienced in keeping time'.

There is plenty of evidence that the Great Western lacked staff, engine power, luggage vans and space: loop lines into which slow trains could be run to allow faster trains to pass; longer platforms – short platforms made trains draw up two or even three times before they could be fully loaded or unloaded; throughout the 1870s milk traffic, in churns, was growing enormously but it was not until 1881 that the Company ran its first milk train.* The Directors wanted punctuality but were not

* See Appendix 2.

prepared – or able – to pay for it. In 1877 the Directors refused
to spend £44 4s 6d on paving the dung-squelchy cattle pens at
Wells with the result that the government health inspector had
them closed and the appalling Somerset & Dorset Railway
carried off the traffic. The Directors were furious, blamed local
officials and ordered Tyrrell down to Somerset to sort matters
out and report to them quickly. The Superintendent of the Line
was not overawed by the Board and his report began: 'There is
nothing to report on' and went on to reprove Their Eminences
very sternly: 'the pens were closed because they were not paved,
work I had recommended to the Board for carrying out but the
Board objected to the cost – £44 4s 6d – and now you are
complaining about the loss of traffic – not that the loss is very
great, this Company took £474 from cattle traffic at Wells last
year.' The cattle pens were duly paved and re-opened.

For all its faults the Great Western Railway inspired great
local loyalty – perhaps this was because it was not perfect but
human; its small stations served their local communities and
did their best for each customer and the public showed their
appreciation at Christmas, individuals demonstrating their
affection with 'Christmas boxes' to the men – a brace of
pheasants or a bottle of brandy, even a sovereign here and there
from the Squire, farmers and traders of the locality; at one
period the gentry and businessmen of Taunton used to band
together to provide the entire station crew with a slap-up
Christmas banquet.

Railwaymen were very partial to social gatherings – they had
the money to buy the beer and there was usually a few men
among the varied staff of lampmen, signalmen, porters,
checkers and carters who could play the piano or deliver a
monologue so a concert party could be raised from time to time
and to these events suitable guests were invited from among the
station's regular customers. Most suitable among these were
the commercial travellers.* These men arrived at each station

* *Privilege Rates for Commercial Travellers, 1890*
The railway companies looked after their considerable trade with these

on their round at regular intervals with their heavy wicker
baskets of samples; indeed, such an important part of the
railway scene were they that the Company gave them cut-price
travel and sometimes organised special trains to take them to
important, rural towns. The travellers arrived and put up at the
Station Hotel, hired a pony and trap and spent one or several
days touring the area, showing samples and taking orders. If the
station staff timed their party correctly they could invite a
traveller dealing in cakes, jam or whisky and he would be sure to
bring some samples along, he might even be a good singer and
thus the quality as well as the quantity of good cheer would be
increased.

Newspaper boys sometimes grew old on a railway platform,
for years crying their hoarse headlines, selling papers to passengers in trains. From the earliest days of railways there had
been W.H. Smith & Son. Smith's were older than the railways
and worked with their motto 'First on the Road'. They used
light carts drawn by powerful teams of horses to rush the
London dailies hot off the presses, round to the great inns from
whence began the inter-city stage-coaches. The object was to
enable anyone willing to pay the subscription to obtain a London
daily 'same day' – anyone within a radius, that is. For far
distant northern or western destinations Smith's carts chased
the stage-coaches which had had to leave London an hour or
two before the papers were printed and, at some pre-arranged
inn, while the horses were being changed, Smith's would catch
up and transfer the precious news. When the railways came
Smith's carts were galloping into the London termini. In 1871
the newspapers for Swansea and west Wales left London on the
6 a.m. Paddington which was fast to Reading and Didcot and

---

travelling salesmen who, in their thousands, rode every railway in the land
with their heavy cases. The GWR declared: 'Commercial travellers' luggage
and their persons are entitled to reduced fares on production of their member-
ship card of their professional association. These persons shall also have
week-end returns at the single rate and will also receive special reductions at
Christmas and Easter to allow them to return home.'

then called at forty of the forty-one stations between Didcot and Swansea (High Street), going via Gloucester and arriving at 3.50 p.m. – if it was on time. On the platform Smith's staff of men and boys stood ready and eager for the fray under the supervision of William Vincent. The papers, bundled in packs of twenty quires, 600 copies, from the various presses, were unceremoniously unloaded, opened and re-made into packs of various papers for wholesalers and retailers; newspapers for individual subscribers such as an iron foundry owner or a country gentleman were wrapped and all the bundles properly addressed. If they were lucky, Vincent's crew had ten minutes to prepare the orders for Carmarthen and beyond, forty minutes to make up the Merthyr consignment and fifty minutes for Llandovery – papers for Swansea and anywhere within a radius of twelve miles waited till last and were delivered by boys with handcarts or on pony-back. The final act of what, to an outsider, would have looked like a free-for-all was a mad gallop of carts piled with packs of newspapers, topped with several 'travelling youths' across the city to Victoria station, London & North Western Railway, for Llandovery and to Riverside station for Merthyr, the trains from both stations leaving at 5 p.m., the former station being one mile from High Street station, the latter two miles. Smith's staff revelled in their skill and knowledge of intricate procedure in getting the orders made up quickly, indeed, the sheer, mad panic of it all was a great, daily excitement – especially when the Great Western arrived late – but it was hardly good business, so Smith's asked if the 6 a.m. could not be speeded up and the Directors, feeling that they had a captive traffic, declined. Smith's knew a thing or two about competition and placed their traffic with the London & North Western Railway. The newspapers were sorted out on the train so that, in spite of the circuitous route to Swansea via Crewe and Shrewsbury and the need to shunt Smith's vans from train to train at those stations, Smith's and the L&NWR were able to deliver the Merthyr and the Llandovery papers on their way down to Swansea and to arrive at the city fifty minutes before the Great Western's service. Now this was extremely serious. The Great Western Directors woke up, prodded Tyrrell and – hey presto – Smith's were promised a 1.45 p.m. arrival at Swansea and Smith's, having made their point, put their traffic back on Great Western metals.

A railway station was even more than the funnel through which practically all the trade and visitors to an area passed; it was, in the days before telephones, the sole source of rapid communication between towns. Before that famous blue and white enamel sign announced 'You may telephone from here' a black and white sign said 'You may telegraph from here'. So important were the railways' telegraph circuits to the nation that in 1868 the Telegraph Act was passed which empowered the Postmaster-General to lease all those wires not directly involved with the operation of the railway in return for a handsome wayleave of 15 shillings a mile of wire.

Tradesmen and Great Men, lacking telephones, used the railway network as a matter of course, even before the 1868 Act and all towns in the country kept 'London time' from the big, 'regulator' clock which hung in main telegraph offices and which was checked daily by the 10 a.m. time signal sent down from Paddington on the electric instruments. W. E. Gladstone was one of many famous men well known to station telegraph clerks and messenger boys up and down the country and, indeed, he called many of them by name as friends. It is recorded that he would send a message from the Oxford telegraph office to London before he boarded the London train, direct that the reply be addressed to the next stopping place – Reading, say – and when he arrived there a messenger boy would be waiting on the platform just where his coach came to a stand with the reply in his hand. The Oxford clerk would ascertain exactly where the great man was sitting and pass on the information.

The Great Western telegraph office at Reading between 1850 and 1896 was a windowless room, 15 ft by 10 ft, beneath the overall roof of the up station, a dark hole and a smelly, not to say dangerous, one. Access was through a frosted glass door from the platform and the customer walked in, facing south towards the town, to a counter just inside, placed narroways across the room. Facing him on the south wall was the 'regulator' clock and hanging beside it was a large horseshoe magnet which might have been used if a relay needed re-polarising. Along the entire 15 ft of the west wall were the telegraph instruments, single- and double-needle types, cased in beautiful, mahogany boxes – although one clerk who worked them believed that the instruments in the South Eastern Railway station just across the way were even more elaborately finished. Above this row of instruments which extended the full length of the wall up to the counter were some gas jets – a plain flame within a glass globe – to provide a poor illumination until the addition of the incandescent mantle in 1905. In front of the instruments sat three clerks on imperfect, three-legged stools, hard at work sending and receiving the messages which were communicated by the left and right deflection of the little, steel needle. They sat with heads bowed over their pads, not watching the needle but listening to its 'tink' and 'tonk' as it struck the tin 'sounders' in response to the movement of a handle by the distant operator. Every other inch of wall space was taken up by the batteries. Shelves in tiers around the walls carried troughs of wood in which stood the 'Daniel' cells – open-topped copper boxes with a small, earthenware vessel within. The inner container held six or eight zinc plates in sulphuric acid to form the cathode; surrounding the earthenware pot was a solution of copper sulphate within the copper tank to form the anode. Dozens of these, wired together, provided the electricity to work the instruments – and worked hard, fizzing and frothing over, spilling a vitriolic mess into the troughs and giving off inflammable hydrogen gas.

Overhead a skylight could let in no light but did perform the vital function of ventilating the explosive gases which was just as well for in the south-east corner of the room a coal fire burnt gaily, casting firelight and flickering shadows about the gloomy

room. It was an impressive, suitably magic atmosphere in
which to find the wonderful electric fluid which – so it was said –
could travel 280,000 miles in one minute even if the wires were
coated in ice. The clerks' great skill in reading off or sending
messages without looking at the flickering needle enhanced the
air of mystery – which would have been explained if the watch-
ers had known that whole sentences, standard questions and
answers were condensed to a single word or letter. Only the
most energetic and quick-witted lads could become clerks and it
is not surprising that several chief officers of the Company
began their careers in the telegraph office.

When costs had to be kept to the minimum, such as the
period between 1865–85, non-profit-making refinements such
as communication between passengers, guard and driver had a
very low priority with the Great Western Directors. But something had to be done. The travelling porter had not been a
success – he tended to coagulate in cold weather and dreadful
incidents sometimes happened which he was quite unable to
prevent, quite apart from the danger of his falling overboard
from time to time. The Public and Parliament demanded some
device – electric or mechanical. The Board saw the need but
hated the idea of spending money or of giving, as they saw it, the
mere passengers any say at all in the running of their trains; on
the other hand, a mechanical contrivance would save the wages
of the travelling porter. The Directors dithered on.

A communication cord would certainly have cut short the
dreadful experience suffered by Mr Chivers and two ladies
which he reported to *Jackson's Oxford Journal* for 29 October
1864. Mr Chivers went to Paddington to take the 11.45 a.m.
'Flying Dutchman' non-stop to Swindon and got into a 2nd class
compartment already occupied by two ladies sitting opposite
each other in corner seats. Soon afterwards a man 'whose
savage face and bloodshot eyes' betrayed his drunken state
tried to enter but Chivers shouted for the guard, the drunk
staggered away and when the guard came up Chivers pointed
the man out and asked the guard, on behalf of the ladies, not to

let him back into their compartment. Just as the train was leaving, the drunk burst into their midst with the guard behind shouting a warning that if he misbehaved he would be left behind on the road. The three genteel passengers huddled furthest from the platform door, with Chivers slightly nearer the man. There they were trapped with this particularly horrid-looking drunk and as for leaving him behind on the road – the train had a ninety-minute, non-stop run to Swindon ahead and they reflected on this miserable fact as they pretended to be absorbed in their books. For a full fifteen minutes the compartment was frigid with embarrassment, the wheels drummed their triple beat, the engine could be heard rasping away at the front, showers of cinders struck the roof with a scratching sound and the drunk's presence was as sore as a burnt eyeball.

As they passed Southall he lurched to his feet, announced that he was a Confederate privateersman and declared himself an enemy of the 'damned English'. Stumbling across to Chivers he knocked his book away and asked what he had to say on the matter. Chivers, hoping to humour him, asked how he came to occupy such an unusual position whereupon the drunk launched into his life's history – how he had gone to Carolina years before and had worked on the plantations as an overseer until the civil war broke out when he set out to make his fortune on the Confederate blockade-runners and privateers. It was a tale of considerable nastiness spiced with oaths and blasphemies and Chivers was glad to be able, eventually, to retreat into his book when the drunk turned back to his corner.

But the man had broken off only to rummage in his bag for a whisky bottle and, having found it, swore loudly that he would 'treat the company'. He swigged down a quarter of the bottle and then presented it to each of the ladies in turn who did their best to melt through the wall into the next compartment so he turned to Chivers and offered a swaying bottle mouth to him, growling that he would 'smash his skylights' if he did not drink to the Confederacy. Chivers pushed the neck of the bottle away and tensed himself for the blow but the man only fell back onto

the seat opposite him and amused himself by alternately swig-
ging and spitting at Chivers' face. When threequarters of the
bottle had gone he fell asleep to the intense relief of the others
who allowed themselves the familiarity of exchanging straight-
into-the-eyes glances of gratitude and commiseration before
sinking wordlessly into their books.

The train kept time to Reading, eased through the yard and
with the engine working hard once more Chivers slipped into a
doze, relaxing to the steady beat of the six-wheeled carriage.
Didcot's point-work shook him awake, he glanced at his watch,
noted that they were now two minutes late and groped for his
book. The drunk was still asleep, sprawling on his back, mouth
open and disgustingly uncouth – but not for much longer. At
Steventon he woke with a snarl or a groan and started to climb
out of the narrow window. The ladies screamed and grabbed
his coat-tails; Chivers leapt to their aid and dragged back on the
man's arm – the other being outside with the other leg. They
pulled and screamed and yelled, the man struggled outwards
and swore frightful blasphemies but, three against one, they
finally dragged him inside and retreated to the far side of the
ten-foot-wide compartment leaving the wretched drunk leaning,
breathless and dishevelled, against the door. He had needed –
desperately – to leave the train and now that he found this
impossible he began to fumble with his fly-buttons. The ladies
screamed in terror, the drunk laughed loud and Chivers just
managed to grab his umbrella and get it open in time to screen
the ladies from this new horror. There was a drumming noise
and a long serpent of evil-smelling water curled across the floor.
The ladies were fainting, the drunk was trying to get round the
umbrella and Chivers tried to pin him to the door with the
ferrule of the umbrella stick. Swindon seemed a very long way
off at that moment and just as Chivers was wondering how long
he could keep the man at bay the engine's brake whistle boomed,
the coaches jostled as they buffered up, the drunk fell over into a
corner seat, speed fell and the train finally came to a stand at
Wantage Road station for an emergency re-fill of the engine's

tender. Chivers stuck his head out of the window, yelled for help and the drunk was carried away, shouting defiance against England and all things English.

After years of protest by the public the communication cord was finally introduced to the Great Western by a reluctant management in August 1869. The cord ran along the outside of the carriages, under the eaves, on the off-side only – a technicality unlikely to be recalled by a panic-stricken traveller in his or her moment of need. Having correctly recalled this fact the alarmed or outraged passenger had then to open the window on its leather strap, reach upwards and grope for the cord, a feat which might well have been impossible for persons of short and/or stout build. The victim then gave the cord several frantic tugs and hoped that the guard had set the lanyard taut enough to operate the engine's whistle or warning gong.

From reading the original circular issued to guards on 1 August 1869 it seems that the cord worked in slightly different ways on broad- and standard-gauge trains. On the latter, the cord was attached either to the brake whistle or to a gong fitted on the tender, close to the cab, and ran from there through guides, to a small wheel high on the inside wall of the rear brake van accommodating the guard. When the guard took over the train he connected the cord throughout and made it as taut as he dared by winding his end of it round the wheel's spindle. He had to leave some slack or else, when the train 'bent' round the sharp curvature of points, the cord would effectively be tightened and thus sound the warning. The adjustment between success and failure was a fine one.

Attached to the spindle of the wheel in the brake van was a bell to jangle when the cord was tugged and every guard had his own, issued bell. At the end of a journey, or before another guard took over the train, the first guard would check to ensure that the system was working correctly and then remove his bell to take it to his next working or to take it home till the next shift – along with his timetable, lamp, flags and detonators. The difference on broad-gauge trains was that the cord rang a bell in the front van and the front guard then pulled a separate cord to operate the warning to the driver.

Slip coaches, which were uncoupled from the rear of a speeding train, were introduced to the Great Western in November 1858 and though the act of uncoupling became a smooth operation involving a lever pulling a wedge out of a hinged draw-hook the original method was very simple. A rope was tied onto the coupling chain and was then brought into the slip guard's compartment through a window in its leading end. At the appropriate spot the engine driver shut off steam to slacken the couplings; the guard, watching for this, lifted the link off the draw-hook and then brought the free-wheeling coach – perhaps with one or two coaches behind – to a stand by means of his handbrake. The system was an immediate success on the Great Western; coaches were dropped off wherever they were needed, provided suitable notice had first been given to signalmen and permanent-way men, the latter being particularly at risk from silent and fast-moving vehicles coming up on them a minute or two after the main train had passed. In fog the practice was even more dangerous and not for nothing was the rule eventually written into the rule-book warning men in charge of level-crossings *not* to put the gates back across the rails until they were certain that the slip coach had passed.

Slip coaches were dropped off trains as a regular part of the schedule – Wantage Road and Twyford had their daily slip coach from 1874 until 1914. At Reading and Taunton the points had to be switched behind the main train and in front of the slip so as to divert the coach into the platform at these 'one-sided' stations. The facing points over which the coach passed were for years moved by a policeman turning a capstan handle without any bolt to hold the blades nor interlocking between the points and the signals. At Ealing a coach was slipped daily in 1864 off an up Bristol express and allowed to run 2½ miles over several set of points without any signalling protection worth speaking of until the guard brought it to a stand at what is now called Old Oak Common where an engine was attached to work it over the west London line, via Addison Road (Kensington), to the Great Western side of Victoria station. Perhaps the most unusual slipping practice of all was off a Windsor to Aldgate train: this was turned onto the Metropolitan Railway's metals at Westbourne bridge and stopped a few hundred yards further on at the Metropolitan's Bishop's Road station, practically an integral part of Paddington station. Off this train a coach was slipped, the Westbourne bridge junction points being turned very smartly to divert the coach into Paddington proper where it arrived two minutes after the main train stopped at Bishop's Road. No doubt this rather dashing, rather dangerous procedure was done for the benefit of the Chairman, the redoubtable, Sir Daniel Gooch.

The slip portions of trains had a communication cord leading to the slip guard's compartment and the cord of the main train came into the compartment through a tube in the leading wall so that, when the slip was made, the main train's cord could draw away smoothly. If the alarm was raised in the slip portion while it was attached to the main train the slip guard passed the message on by tugging on the 'main train' cord hoping, literally, 'to hit the bell' on the engine 50 or 80 yds away. If there were two slips and the alarm was raised in the rear slip then the rear slip guard tugged the front slip's cord and the front slip guard tugged the 'main train' cord; up to three slip portions could be towed on the rear of a train. The cord worked – more or less – but the Board of Trade, after giving their approval to it in 1869 withdrew approval in 1873. The outside cord remained in use until 1900.

So the passengers travelled in their lavatory-less, unheated (except for tins of hot water), non-corridor trains, lit by an oil lamp or two per compartment. The better-off passengers came well prepared with blankets, food and a little, medicinal, brandy for almost any journey was a long one, none too warm in the best weather, chilling in ordinary rain and a potential death-trap in real cold. The great blizzards of 1881 and 1888 came with such bitter cold that ink froze on pens and the Smith's news-stand man kept a candle burning so he could thaw his pen nib at intervals. Somehow, in some way as yet unexplained, the engine crews and indeed the passengers survived the arctic temperatures – and the enginemen were on cab-less or next to cab-less engines. The cuttings filled with snow, the open track was buried in huge drifts and all trains – even those hauled by the big, 4-4-0 'Waverley' class broad-gauge engines – were brought to a stand and rapidly buried under drifting snow.* In Moreton cutting, just east of Didcot, a 'Waverley' was buried for four days before the gangs dug their way through to it and in all that time the driver or fireman had stood by it, taking the self-imposed duty in shifts between them.

The telegraph offices became the centres for co-ordinating the rescue operation – the benefits of electric communication, by 1888, having firmly impressed themselves on the official mind and George Tyrrell, the seventy-two-year-old Superintendent of the Line spent 48 hours continuously on duty in Reading telegraph office until the ice-laden wires finally collapsed in the raging blizzard. The Thames valley suffered an arctic 'white-out'.

A Birmingham to Paddington train arrived at Oxford, took on a few passengers including a seventeen-year-old girl travelling alone to Didcot and resumed its southward journey until, five miles further on, it was brought to a stand in deep snow. The girl, unprepared for a long journey – her top coat was none too warm – heard voices outside and unwisely dropped her window. The blizzard screamed in. Barely visible, ten feet away

---

* The GWR kept snowploughs at all main centres – Gloucester, Oxford, Shrewsbury, Hereford, Worcester, Wolverhampton, Swindon and so on – in order that the main lines should be kept free of drifting snow. It was not possible to provide such insurance for the hundreds of miles of single track branch lines and these had to take their chance. The Company felt this lack, this loophole, keenly and to satisfy its corporate conscience issued such lines as the Much Wenlock branch with strict instructions: 'During snow storms the branch engine is to run up and down the line to keep it clear.' Totally unrealistic though this was, the Superintendent felt he had done what he could and left the rest to the good sense and determination of his men.

on the track were two workmen up to the thighs in snow.

'Are we snowed up?' she asked timidly.

'Stuck fast, Miss,' came the laconic reply.

'We all ought to turn to and help clear the way,' she said bravely.

'Aha! If they was all like you, Miss, we should soon have you on your way.'

The men moved away, she pulled up the window and sat down. She was plastered in snow, snow covered the floor, the minutes dragged an hour past and then another; the wind blew powdery snow in through cracks around the door; the compartment, darkened by snow clogging the windows, grew darker as the short day ended till she sat in darkness, cold and growing colder, hungrier than she would have thought possible. Her feet were painfully cold but, being quite alone, she felt she could safely take off her shoes to rub her toes; this she did and then lay down on the seat close to tears, her head pillowed on her shawl, melting snow making the neck and wrists of her dress wet and icy cold. In her lonely cell, with no sound but the howling gale, she drifted into a dangerous sleep.

Shouts and bangs on the carriage door woke her. Her numb feet hurt as she struggled to stand up. 'Anyone in there?' The door was dragged open from outside to show a crowd of shadowy figures, Radley college boys, workmen and villagers, carrying lanterns and spades. The man who opened the door climbed in. 'Come on, Miss, I'll hand you down to the others. You'll be all right – it's only a step to the station.'

NINE

Swindleum Station

On 23 September 1841 it dawned gloriously over the Cotswolds, the sun shining through a thin mist, turning it into a golden veil, then, drying it, shone on fields golden with stubble and stooked wheat, hillsides brilliant green, dotted with sheep. Cirencester crackled with excitement and the sound of iron-shod tyres on cobbles as elegant phaetons from Cheltenham, omnibuses from Gloucester and farm carts full of locals converged and jostled through the streets making for the railway station. The line from Swindon had opened a few weeks before and a Cheltenham man had had the bright idea of chartering a train to carry a thousand people to London and back in a day. The fare was 13s 6d a head, hundreds had taken up the offer and so Cirencester was full of people, sightseers and those actually travelling; there were cheers from by-standers when some especially dashing conveyance cantered in, shouts of 'Which way to the rail-road?' answered by shouted directions from locals whose breasts swelled with feelings of importance – and a great deal of bugling on copper coach-horns. On both sides of the railway line the crowds gathered to see the start of this unique undertaking until thousands thronged the banks all the way to Kemble tunnel, four and a quarter miles away.

At the head of the long train in Cirencester station stood *Hecla,* a 'two-four-nought' type specially chosen for the job on account of being brand new and having 5-ft driving wheels – a slow, powerful machine. The 850 passengers settled themselves into their none-too-comfortable carriages and at 11.30 the wonderful journey got under way. The train stopped at several stations to refresh the engine, passengers leaped out for fresh stocks of beer, excitement in the packed train was infectious, the day was fine and many passengers became uproariously drunk as the train progressed eastwards at speeds in excess of 30 mph. The news of its approach – a train bearing nearly a thousand Gloucestershire provincials and rustics – arrived at Paddington well before it and a large number of very choice specimens of the London underworld gathered at the terminus to reap this harvest so considerately provided by the Great Western Railway.

Such a Metropolitan welcome! Thirty of the trippers, very merry, clambered on board an omnibus intent on seeing the sights, and were joined by a heavily built man, not one of the excursionists for he was dressed in deep mourning with a face to match. He sat, apparently inconsolable, amongst the jolly country folk until he had somewhat dampened their feelings and made his presence known whereupon he gave a heart-broken cry and fell to the floor. The kindly rustics called for the omnibus to be stopped and all tried to help the poor man to rise. He was heavy and rolled about considerably till just about everyone had had a go at lifting him, then, like a conjuror, he had stepped off the 'bus onto the pavement and was lost in the crowd. The omnibus drove on. Only when the Gloucestershire men and women came to take out their purses did they realise they had been robbed.

Excursions very soon became part of the railway scene and were hugely popular, allowing, as the Duke of Wellington had gloomily foretold, the lower classes to move about. A train from Steventon to Weymouth, in 1853, called at all stations to Swindon and left the Junction made up to thirty-eight carriages hauled by three engines and this, in early days, till the practice was forbidden by the Board of Trade, was not an isolated incident. The Great Western never seemed to have any trouble in providing trains of extra carriages for 'the people' – even though it disliked carrying the lower classes on its regular trains – and this is far more than can be said for the nationalised railway now.

When the Great Western got over its dislike of 'persons of the lower orders' sufficiently to provide seating for them on regular trains quite lowly persons made their own, individual excursions. In 1850 or thereabouts, one Tom Plowman was a carter from the village of Coln St Aldwyn, near Cirencester. He was in love with a girl from the village, Sarah Jane, who was away in London 'in service' as a lady's maid, so Tom took the momentous decision to go all the way to London to see her. The village was agog and the general opinion was that 'he would be murdered before he came back'. But Tom was in love and determined. 'Rest easy in yer mind,' he told Sarah's mother, who was cook at the Manor. 'I'm toughish and I'll see the honour of the old county is kep' up.' He set out early on Monday to walk the ten miles to Cirencester and was very pleased with the handsome shops around the square but quite delighted with the magnificent church standing, towering, over them. 'Didn't look as how the church were built by the same sort o' folk who built the shops,' he said later. Passing through the square he came to the railway station, walked into the booking hall and found a queue of people taking their turn at a small window in the wall, pushing their money through and getting a small rectangle of pasteboard back. When Tom's turn came he bent low to speak at the little window and asked, 'Will you take I ter Lunnon?'

'First, second or third?' asked the man behind the glass.

'Fust, o' course,' replied Tom scornfully. 'Fust – not arter – Sarah Jane will be a-waitin'.'

'That will be twenty-five shillings then,' said the booking clerk with lofty disdain.

Tom's face darkened – he had been warned against railwaymen, and he was toughish. 'Parson said as how it would only be eight shillin',' he replied threateningly.

'That's third class then,' said the clerk, 'and you'll be in London the same time as the rest.'

Somewhat bewildered Tom paid his fare, took his pasteboard ticket and went out to join the train. Off it went faster than racehorses and Tom, still distrustful of the clerk, asked his fellow passengers where they were going. 'Cheltenham', said one; 'Bristol', said another; 'South Wales', said a third. 'Dang the button o' that little pasteboard seller!' thought Tom. 'I'll black his eye when I gets home for putting me on the wrong train.' Out loud he asked, with some anger, 'How be we all to get where we're a-goin' – all on one train?' The others laughed and instructed him in the techniques of junctions and changing trains. Next his attention was caught by the sight of all the telegraph wires strung from poles all along the lineside. 'Do the Great Western take in a lot of washing as well as running trains?' he asked innocently.

Never had he travelled so fast or so far through places so different from his own, secluded, Coln St Aldwyn. Through a tunnel, a deep cutting, over a tall embankment for miles past houses built in red brick, seeing different styles of thatching, till at last the train curved slowly into Swindon Junction station past the enormous factory, a town in itself, full of men all of whom seemed to Tom to be as black as sweeps, to the platform where green-liveried porters announced 'All Change' and the departure of the train for Paddington in fifteen minutes. Tom got out and followed a crowd through double doors into a large room where people were eating at tables and some very good-looking girls were serving food from behind a massive, mahogany counter. Tom strode up to them, feeling peckish.

'I'll have half a quartern loaf,' he said firmly.

'We don't keep a baker's shop,' replied one pretty young lady, primly. 'There's cake, biscuits, sliced bread and meat.'

'Have yer got some bacon – rather fattish?'

'No – but there's some good pork sausages at sixpence.'

'Hand over the plate, young 'ooman,' ordered Tom, in his 'man of the world' voice, 'and I'll trouble you fer the mustard an' salt an' that ther plate of bread an' butter.'

With a loaded plate in each, huge, hand, he strode to a table and sat down to eat his snack. The sausages were very good but the bread was cut so thin he had to put four slices together just to make a mouthful. He had no need of a knife and fork but the young lady behind the counter, watching at work, brought him a beautiful, ivory-handled steel knife and solid silver fork and laid them down by his plate with a sniff and a toss of her head. Tom picked them up, admired them and put them down, they were far too small for his farm-labourer's hands. He ran out of bread half-way through the sausages so he called for another plate and was getting on wonderfully when he felt the need for a drink. 'Young 'ooman!' he called across the room, 'have 'ee got summat as would wet my whistle? A quart of ale p'r'aps?'

As he called the whistle sounded from an engine and through the windows he saw the London train moving away. Still with a sausage in his hand he rushed to the door, out onto the platform. 'Oi! Wait fer I,' he shouted waving his sausage in the air, 'Sarah Jane will be waitin' in Lunnon.' The porters laughed at him: 'You'll have plenty of time to finish them sausages now, Mr Turmot.'

Back in the refreshment room went Tom to find the young lady had brought out a tall bottle with a thick rim at the top of the neck. Tom was really thirsty now so he knocked the neck off the bottle, cracking it on the rim of the table – and the contents shot foaming over the party seated opposite.

'Hey!' shouted Tom in great alarm.

'How dare you, sir! yelled the gentleman as champagne squirted all over his wife. The wicked young lady hurried round from behind the counter. 'Oh, what have you done?'

Tom was furious and butted in. 'I arsked fer ale – this ere ain't ale.'

'That was Moses champagne at seven and six a bottle.'

'That was just a lot of pop, Miss,' said Tom defiant and embarrassed, out of his depth with all eyes on him and quite a few sniggers, too, directed at him.

'That'll be thirteen shillings – sir,' said the pretty assistant putting her nose in the air.

'Thirteen shi . . .! What for?'

The girl folded her arms aggressively. 'Seven sausages, three and sixpence, twenty four slices of bread and butter, two shillings, and a bottle of Moses champagne, seven and six, comes to thirteen shillings.'

Tom was aghast and angry too – these railway people were out to make a fool of him. 'You told me as how the sausage were sixpence an' the bread off a tuppenny loaf.'

'The sausage are sixpence each and the bread is a penny a slice,' said the girl impatiently, her voice rising to match Tom's.

'Do 'ee call that reasonable, young 'ooman?' asked Tom, ' 'cause I aint a-goin' ter pay thirteen shillings for two or three sausingers, a few bits o' bread and a bottle of pop – not if I knows it.' He towered over her, as broad as Gloucestershire, and the other customers grinned at his innocence.

The double doors swung open and a top-hatted policeman came striding in through the tables, the porter who had summoned him scurrying along behind. The peeler came to a stand before Tom, his top hat level with the brim of Tom's bowler. 'Be you a-goin' to pay fer what you've had?' he demanded briskly.

'O' course I am,' replied Tom. 'Here's sixpence fer the sausages, tuppence for the bread, tuppence fer the pop – and a shilling fer the young 'ooman as served me, just to show there's no hard feelings.'

'You 'ad thirteen shillings' worth o' grub an' if you don't pay I'll take you away and lock you up.'

Tom grinned down at him cheerfully. 'Do 'ee think as how you could do all that, my man? No disrespect to 'ee but I could catch hold of the scruff of your neck and the seat of your breeches and pitch you out into the road amongst the iron.'

The policeman drew his painted truncheon and said with an air of great finality. 'Look 'ere, Master Hodge, there's plenty here to carry you off – so pay what you owes or London won't hold you tonight.'

Tom knew when he was beaten, so he threw down the rest of his money, all he had on him, shoved the policeman aside and stormed to the door. 'You calls this Swindon station,' he shouted at the exit. 'I calls it *Swindleum* station. Be dammed to you all! He stormed out and had to take the next train home having no money left for his trip to Paddington.

Excursions trains in the nineteenth century consisted of the worst carriages available; in 1870 the Great Western branded and categorised their carriages:

Ⓔ E O X

Ⓔ stock was supposed to be the very best, kept exclusively for the west of England expresses; E was for all other expresses and for strengthening the west of England trains; O stock was for ordinary stopping trains; and X stock was 'Excursion only – never to be used in regular trains'. Events did not work quite so well, an E coach might end up on the St Erth – St Ives branch, much to the delight of the passengers or an Ⓔ carriage, taken out of an express for repairs might be replaced by an O and, thus modified, the train could run for a week before a letter from an irate 1st class passenger to the General Manager at Paddington, complaining of the rough ride or lack of 1st class accommodation, would alert the Company and thus get matters put right. As traffic built up the railwaymen's job became increasingly complicated and while they did their best, the means at their disposal were always limited; carriages, communications and siding space were always in short supply.

There were procedures for everything by 1890 but they depended on the men having the time to carry them out – rather like the situation on British Rail today concerning the computerisation of wagon movements. At Malvern Link station on 3 June 1892 a horse-box was shunted off an up passenger train into the horse dock. The horse was unloaded and the vehicle cleaned out thoroughly after which the porter ought to have 'wired' the Wagon Inspector at Worcester, using the single-needle telegraph instrument, to ask for disposal instructions. What he actually did was rather more direct. He labelled the horse-box 'Wagon Inspector, Worcester' and put it on the next up stopping train, which went to Worcester; job done, nothing more to worry about. When the train arrived at Worcester the shunters took the box off the rear of the train which was going on to London and, as they had no use for it nor had the time to go and ask the Wagon Inspector what he wanted to do with it, they took it, still attached to the little, shunting, saddle tank and stuck it on the rear of a train for Shrewsbury via the Severn Valley line. Shrewsbury did not want it just at that moment and sent it down to Hereford. All this was wasted wear, tear and fuel consumption it was also fairly typical of the situation on the Great Western at the time because a stern notice was issued later in 1892 part of which stated: 'There are far too many vehicles wandering empty about the system.'

Bank holidays placed a terrific strain on the Company's stock; every coach fit or even unfit to turn a wheel was pressed into service and still huge crowds accumulated on such stations as Birmingham, Paddington and Bristol, all expecting – as of right – that there would be a train to take them to their favourite sea-side resort: 'Brummagem-super-Mare' or Weymouth – 'Swindon-by-the-Sea'. The crush, rush, panic and delay of Bank Holiday travel was legendary through generations and the earlier the period the greater the fuss because then people were less sophisticated, had less understanding of the system and were far more independent of thought and action. Where did people queue before the advent of railway booking offices? Probably only at the workhouse gates or the gin-shop door; the railways' organisation took a bit of getting used to. Whit Monday 1891 was fine and warm in Bristol, huge crowds were expected at Temple Meads station and, as a booking clerk at the station that day later recorded, they arrived. A group of thirty 'Strict Wesleyans' methodically purchased their tickets to Weston-super-Mare in advance, choosing the first train out and thereby hoping to avoid the crowds and delays that later trains and travellers would suffer. They overslept, arrived at the station too late and had a most un-Christian row with an innocent platform inspector.

Those proceeding in the conventional way arrived at Temple Meads half an hour before their train to find a raggle-taggle regiment of two hundred or so trippers ahead of them, the men a bit beery, mothers with their tempers fraying a little at the edges and cheeky or bored children, all shuffling very slowly towards the far distant ticket windows and all fiercely jealous of their place in the queue. Frustration broke down inhibition and perfect strangers spoke to one another, comparing past experiences, scorning the Great Western's miserable performance and alluding to the glories of the South Western or the North Western – especially when any Great Western staff came near.

Some people became very nervous about missing their train; an engine's whistle blew and three friends, without really thinking, darted up to the ticket gate to see if it was their train that was moving off and were none the wiser for seeing a rake of coaches pulling away. They returned to their places in the queue but the queue had closed the gap, everyone was three places nearer the ticket window, the queue closed up tight – chests to backs – and stared stonily ahead. Wiser about human nature the three trooped off sadly to the back of the line.

At the ticket window the Bristol booking clerk who left his account of this day had to switch his brains about issuing all kinds of different tickets to all kinds of people – the stupid, the timid and the just plain dishonest. Into which category this dear old Somersetshire lady fits, I leave the reader to decide. She came to the ticket window and in her rich, slow, Somerset voice asked for 'Two to Weston please, my 'usband will be 'ere to pay thee just as soon as he gets back from locking up the fowls.'

'I've heard that one before,' grinned the clerk. 'You look after your fowls and I'll look after my wife and family.'

The wide platforms under the cavernous roof were full of hurrying, bewildered people, a train arrived and the crowd surged forward, often sweeping into it those who did not wish to go to that destination. The porters did what they could by crying 'Weymouth train' or whatever but passengers often preferred to ask those already seated where the train was going and with so many trippers out for a lark on a rare day off work this was not wise. Yet others knew all about railways and could fend for themselves – such as one Father who, with wife and brood, were off to Weston for the day. The porters were calling 'Weston train' but observant Father had seen that the engine had a curved, brass, destination board alongside the boiler which quite plainly stated 'Wolverhampton' – he was not going to be caught like that. And the train went to Weston without them. As the trains filled they were flagged away and all the passengers thrilled to the first, exciting movements – they were off, off to the sea! Past marshalling yards and back gardens, out into the country where the novelty wore off and boredom crept in. At Castle Cary station, where a mass of flowers graced the length of both platforms, an excursion from Birmingham to Weymouth ground to a halt with the signals against it. There followed a longish wait during which many of the male trippers took the opportunity of relieving themselves in the little, cast-iron lavatory on the down platform and mothers took young children behind bushes. A young lad picked a bunch of flowers for his mother, then another, Birmingham was short on flowers, the idea caught on, a rose bush was dug up and taken into the carriage – and all this screened from the view of the station office on the up platform until the signals cleared and the train drew aside to reveal the devastation to the porters opposite. Man-traps and spring-guns were judged too humane for such vandals and they telegraphed a warning down the line.

Trains also queued. The train carrying the horticultural enthusiasts was following behind several others and was stopped again at Sparkford where two nine-gallon casks of beer caught the eyes of an eager group of Brummies. Out they got, quick, and were just lifting the second cask into their den when the porters, alerted by the signalman – who had got the message from Castle Cary – came storming over the footbridge. Then it was 'Names and addresses, please!' One man was 'John Brown of Nowhere' and the other was his brother living just across the street but then the signals were lowered so the casks were retrieved and the train moved off, saving all concerned a great deal of bother. Having arrived at Weymouth the train disgorged its 700 passengers and retired to sidings. The day had fulfilled its early promise and was sunny, almost hot. The station staff looked after the hurrying battalion of Brummies as they stormed into the trembling Dorset town. 'That's the last we'll see o' they till nightfall, thank the Lord,' they said to each other. They were wrong. Two hours later a group of about two hundred very drunk excursionists were back on the station, their singing hollow under the high roof, waving bottles of ale. They had had their spree and wanted to go home.

Return excursions were more chaotic than forward journeys because no matter how many return trains there were, most trippers wanted their day to last as long as possible so they tended all to crowd into the latest train home. Excursion carriages had only oil-lamps – or no lamps – in each compartment and at a signal stop at some wayside station in the deepening, summer dusk the occupants of one twilit compartment called to the Station Master, 'Bring us a light – it's dark in here.' Only an aged porter was on duty, he came creaking across the platform and offered to give them his box of matches. The customers took great offence. 'Best oi can do zur,' he said apologetically – and it was too but they still wrote a letter to the Bristol paper, complaining about the old boy's 'impudence'.

The best-organised excursion in Britain, with the most railway-knowledgeable passengers, took place each year during July/August when approximately half the population of a large town was, in the space of a few hours, carried away on holiday in trains provided free of charge by the Company. This was Swindon Mechanics' Institute Annual Trip, which began as a day's excursion and grew into a fortnight's holiday. It was known simply as 'Trip' – a legend to this day among many Swindonians, an annual triumph of operating carried out with practised precision by the railwaymen. Nor was this the only gigantic outing which Swindon railwaymen, through the Company, organised. Each year there was the Great Western Railway fête when the Company laid on a full-size fair with swings and gallopers, tea, buns and fruit cake. Each railway child was allowed one free ride on the sixpenny gallopers and all railwaymen and their families were given a free cup of tea and piece of fruit cake. The cake was baked by the hundredweight and nothing less than the Territorial Army drill hall was big enough to accommodate the cake-cutting operation as dozens of railway wives stood at rows of trestle tables, hacking away at the dark, curranty – GWR designed – fruit cake.

'Trip' was the only long holiday of the year and was very eagerly awaited – especially by the children and weeks beforehand they were chalking on walls, all round the town: ROLL ON TRIP. It was like Christmas with an equally long and unbearable Advent during which many children saved 'Trip money', their little columns of coppers rising like barometers of excitement. As the time grew near it became, if not the sole topic of conversation, at least the opening gambit – 'Where y'goin' Trip?' – superseding even the weather for general, all-consuming interest Shops sold 'Trip bargains' or 'Trip bonnets' – anything to make as much as they could out of the growing excitement, as well they might for once the trains had left, the town was a ghost town until they returned.

On Monday or Tuesday evening of 'Trip week' the whole family might crowd round the kitchen table to watch the first significant move towards the long-awaited holiday: the filling-in of the Privilege Ticket order form. Next day one of or all the children of the family took the 'priv form' to the Works booking office, queuing with many others to exchange the paper slips for the precious little rectangles of stiff card – the key to sandy beaches and blue, far distant, hills.

How wonderful 'Aberystwyth' looked, how mysterious, on the little green card as the excited children examined the ticket on the way home through Emlyn Square – even 'Weymouth' looked pretty good. 'You 'ent goin' there agen?' said the superior Aberystwyths. The tickets had then to be put 'somewhere safe' against the Day – up on the dresser, in the old tea caddy – and still today one can hear dreadful stories of those terrible moments, long ago when, at three in the morning, just as the whole family was about to leave, Father finally admitted that he could not remember where he had put the ticket.

I have no details of the 1892 operation but 'Trip' was the same, year after year, except that the numbers grew larger. In 1903 22,500 men, women and children travelled in twenty-one special trains. Swindon could provide only a fraction of the stock and motive power requirements; 300 carriages and 15 locomotives came into sidings east and west of Swindon station from places as far apart as Plymouth, Carmarthen and Paddington, arriving at intervals between 10 p.m. on Thursday and 4 a.m. on Friday. The engines went to shed for coal, water and, if necessary, to turn and while they were away the coaches they had brought were re-marshalled, labled, watered, lamped and generally made ready for the horde so that when the engine returned in something under two hours its train was ready and sometimes even loaded-up for the run to Weymouth, Penzance or Carmarthen – or any of a dozen destinations – the longer-distance trains getting away earliest. The marshalling and the loading was done mainly in Rodbourne Lane sidings, outside the factory, thus avoiding interfering with the regular work of Swindon station and to do this, the planners assumed – depended on – the good railway sense of all concerned and their knowledge of local, railway geography so that no one got lost in the maze of darkened sidings or run over by shunting engines as thousands converged on the trains.

The travellers were up very early, waking – if they had slept at all – to the beautiful realisation that this was *it*. Trip Friday had arrived. All over Swindon and even out in the villages (special trains were run in from Purton) doors opened and into the familiar streets, mysteriously unfamiliar in the dark, skipped the children, their parents following with bags and baggage, including presents for relations – one brave soul carrying a potted geranium ever hopeful that it would survive the scrum and arrive intact. The streets streamed, converging into a flood of laughing trippers, calling to workmates. Trip bonnets bobbing alongside stiff, Trip suits and creaky-new, Trip shoes. Then the excitement of the walk along the pitch-dark track – with mothers desperately trying to keep a track of their children in the press – the scramble up off the ballast into the coaches, the first, wonderful surge of the 'Off', later to see the sun rise over some distant county and finally to see the sea.

A whole week of doing nothing, listening to the roar of the waves instead of the insane hammer of the riveting guns, bright sun and fresh air instead of the gloom and smoke of the iron foundry – a different beer than Ansell's in a pub other than the Cricketers until the carefully hoarded money had been spent and it was time to board the Trip specials back to Swindon and the reality of two lean weeks – because holidays were then without pay; the Friday following their return, which would otherwise have been pay-day, was known as 'Black Friday', when 10,000 men streamed glumly past the Works pay office in what was sardonically called the 'Grand March Past'.

TEN

The Great Western Revived

'No man may become an engine driver on any other terms but fearless toil,' said a Locomotive Inspector sternly during a lecture to the Swindon Mechanics' Institute in 1900. When a Gooch 8-ft 'Single' went huffing quietly off shed, sleeker than a racehorse, there were often still clinging to it, like a swarm of grimy bees, the gang of cleaning lads giving it their final, fussing, polish. The Great Western, following on from Brunel's 1838 admonition to R. W. Hawthorn Ltd, provided their drivers with the utmost in mechanical excellence, gave every component the most satisfying shape and dressed each loco-motive in such a livery of brass, copper and paint so that he felt proud of his engine, proud of his own skill and toughness in being a Great Western Railway Engineman and every cleaner-boy desired above all else to become a driver and have charge of one of these magnificent machines.

There was some controversy among broad- and 'narrow'-gauge drivers as to who had the best engines and as the broad gauge became confined entirely to west of England trains the sense of uniqueness grew, the feeling that driving Gooch eight-footers was special – which it was. The Company reinforced this view by noting in official records that 'So and so has been "transferred to the broad gauge" ' where they received the close attention of the Chairman of the Board whose engines they were driving. Some narrow-gauge men resented their prestige; the old broad-gauge 'Singles' were out-classed by 1870, let alone 1890; they could not keep time with their trains – which was hardly their drivers' fault – but still the official view was that the broad gauge was somehow superior and with Gooch as Chairman this is hardly surprising. However, Robert Duff, a driver who had never had anything to do with the broad gauge, fiercely resented broad-gauge prestige and believed that men who had worked only the 7-ft gauge were incapable of driving standard-gauge engines successfully. Duff was an ace driver who began on the Shrewsbury & Chester Railway – a wholly narrow-gauge affair – which was absorbed into the Great Western, and Duff with it, in 1854. In June 1860 he resigned and went driving in Egypt but something went wrong with his plans because he re-applied for employment on the Great Western at Shrewsbury in 1862 and was accepted. In November 1868 he was ordered to Oxford but refused, stating as his reason: 'I will not work with ex-broad-gauge men on narrow-gauge engines.' He maintained his prejudice in spite of one week's loss of pay and loss of his annual bonus but he was far too valuable a man to lose; the Great Western allowed him to stay at Shrewsbury and in October 1888 he became Shed Foreman at Corwen.

A boy had to toil hard even to become a cleaner of the Gooch 'Singles' and having been promoted to such a cleaning gang he had first to work on their tenders or underneath the engine, among the valve rods, before he was allowed to polish the boiler and finally the brass, copper and bright steel handrails, couplings and buffer heads. This was the training ground for the drivers of the future who had to be very tough men simply to survive the elements; this was where the boys learned the rudiments of how the engine worked and developed a feeling of belonging to the team. The job was filthy and hard but the results were very satisfying and with this went the promise of a lifetime of work – if you could stand the pace – and if you could stand several years as a cleaner you could probably stand anything.

Of their pride in results there can be little doubt, given a certain amount of 'driving' by the Chargehand. Many gangs on a regular rota of, say, four engines, made 'clothing' out of sacks which fitted over the brass dome, safety-valve cover and boiler top to protect these parts from soot and the tarnishing effect of smoke inside the shed. The shining effect of their efforts – checked for dirt by the Foreman's white handkerchief – remains for all to see in the photographs of the period.

White corduroy clothing for enginemen gave way to a motley garb during the 1870s when 'whites' were mixed with black worsted jacket, trousers and waistcoat and topped off with a variety of headgear – soft caps, flat caps, 'pork pie' hats and bowler hats – any of which were pulled down hard over the brows of the wearer when they were out on the line at speed. By the late 1880s some kind of uniformity emerged as the engines began to take on an ultimate smartness: some drivers appeared in a cloth-topped peaked cap of regulation design with the famous collarless jacket which it was *de rigueur* to wear buttoned tight around the throat by a single button to allow the rest to fall open, exposing the ample corporation decorated with watch-chain and fob; each driver bought his own watch, the most expensive he could afford, and some were very expensive chronometers – the Great Western issued only their guards with watches. These grand old drivers stare out at one from the ancient photographs, some looking like jolly pirates with their outrageous beards and motley dress, others are stern, full of feelings of 'fearless toil' – but one and all a tough, independent, weatherbeaten crew, clutching their highly polished, 'long feeder' oil cans just as a naval officer of the period would lean upon his sword.

On the road, in the days of white corduroys, disc-and-crossbar signals and the time-interval system of signalling, drivers may well have felt that 50 mph was a good maximum speed to ensure that their hats stayed on their heads and that their heads stayed on their shoulders. The wonder is that there were so few accidents – due partly to having fewer trains running, but mainly to the intense concentration on the driver's part as he stared ahead into the wind, with sore eyes, looking for the next signal which at night would be no more than a small red or white light.

At Heyford, between Oxford and Banbury, one evening in 1852, an up stopping train arrived; the policeman turned the red light on behind it, walked along to the station to enter the time in his register and then helped the station staff with the passengers.

As he emerged from the office the Station Master was heard by several passengers to say, 'There's that horse-box over in the goods shed – set the road and we'll back the train over to fetch it.'

The policeman first walked out to the down disc-and-crossbar signal and turned it to 'Danger' before walking back to the crossover and siding points which he altered for the crossing movement, switching the blades round by his ground levers. The train then backed across from the up to the down main to the goods shed where it came to a stand with the rear coach buffered against the horse-box but with the engine just 'foul' of the down main line. While the policeman had been walking out to the down signal a down express train was approaching though still a mile away. The track fell downhill and the driver was letting his train run at nearly 60 mph, he was very sure of himself and knew exactly where, in the dark, to look to catch the earliest glimpse of Heyford's signal – over there, through those trees, across the invisible curve of the line. There it was, a small, strong, white light. He watched it until it became obscured. The train was 900 yds away. At 450 yds the signal came fully into view. It was at 'Danger'. The driver blew for the guard's brake and put the engine into reverse while his mate frantically screwed the tender handbrake down. They had no chance of pulling-up and hit the engine of the stopping train – though at a considerably reduced speed. The driver of the fast train jumped off just before the impact and impaled himself on a point lever whilst his fireman stayed with the engine and survived.

When a white light indicated 'All Right' – and this was a situation which the Company did not even start to alter until 1895 – it was, in theory at least, possible for a driver to be misled by a candle in the window of a house or by a street lamp on a bridge close to a signal. Imagine driving into a town's station at night – even driving through it at speed – your guiding white lights mingled with false lights, a platform lamp standing in front of a signal (there is no perspective at night), you cannot see which way the line curves, the white light ahead is not on the track at all, the track curves round to the left and your signals are over there. A driver and his fireman had to know the precise number of signals at each station and exactly where to look for them over a hundred miles of track.

Yet in spite of a signalling system years behind the development of locomotive power the drivers drove into pitch darkness at up to 80 mph. More than any other grade they were open to the most searching supervision. Each was held responsible for his engine's daily maintenance by other men and for his fireman's work; each ensured it was properly oiled, that steam glands were steam-tight, that the fireman had steam up at the proper time – a driver could be fined for any failing of the fireman's. For this reason the driver was truly the captain of his ship, on the footplate his word was law, yet, according to the rule book he was subordinate to the guard and to all Station Masters so that it was not unknown by any means for a driver to be reported for not blowing his whistle as he approached a station, which was worth a 2s 6d fine, as well as being liable to punishment after a bad report from a fitter or shed foreman. Against this it must also be said they were highly valued by the Company; a man could have a list of 'offences' as long as his arm – many did – but they still obtained their promotion and often became foremen. Promotion was in fact obligatory – an automatic function of seniority. It was quite normal for a man to do something dreadful like allow his fireman to burn the boiler and then to hit him out of sheer frustration and for him then to be promoted the following week. Dismissal – on the Great Western at any rate – was by no means frequently used nor was it the automatic punishment for theft and drunkenness as might be imagined.

My great-grandfather, Francis Cook, became an engine

cleaner on the Great Western Railway at Chippenham shed in March 1875 aged fourteen and shortly before his seventeenth birthday he had become a 3rd class fireman earning 3s 6d a day. He was obviously a smart, capable lad but the sudden wealth of wages went to his head and he began drinking, not heavily but enough to become known as a bit of a rake around Chippenham and Calne. He began courting my great-grandmother, Catherine Day, from Calne, who was eighteen months older than him so he was obviously full of confidence in himself, just the sort of man to become an engine driver. Catherine was obviously smitten by the dashing and carefree Francis and turned a blind eye to his more boisterous ways. Catherine worked as a lady's maid at a big house called The Quarry in Calne, her employer was very fond of her and took upon herself the duty of warning her against marrying Francis: 'If you can't change him before you are married, you certainly will not afterwards.' The famous words were handed down our family through the years.

Francis became a 2nd class fireman at Bristol in June 1884, earning 4 shillings a day and worked from Bath Road shed mainly on long-haul, night goods work. He married Catherine in August that year and they moved to a house in Totterdown high above the Bath Road engine sheds with a magnificent view over Bristol. The wedding celebrations were of a somewhat strenuous nature for he overstayed his leave from the railway by three days for which he was reported as 'Absent without leave' and fined £2. Catherine now knew what she was in for. Their first child was born ten months later, child followed child and her housekeeping money had to be stretched further while he boozed away the lion's share. When things got really bad she had to go down to the gates of the shed on pay days and take the money off him there and then before he could get into the pub, which was right outside the engine shed gate. That strategem worked until November 1889 when he became a 1st class fireman at 4s 9d a day, working from Taunton. He travelled to and from his new depot and was out of reach of Kate on pay days. His minor and major misdemeanours, all brought on by his drinking or his bad temper when he could not get a pint, meant even less money at home for six children and their mother.

In April 1891, at the second attempt, he passed his driving examination, medical and practical, and was posted to Southall as a 3rd class driver. He was on the pilot one day at Slough when a main line goods stopped so that its fireman, who had been on long hours, could take rest – the fireman off Francis Cook's engine going onto the goods and a cleaner lad coming out of the shed for the pilot. Perfectly normal and straightforward except that Francis refused to lose his fireman. The cleaner came out but Francis sent him back with a message for the Foreman: 'No cleaners on my engine.' He absolutely refused so other arrangements were made and Francis was fined 2 shillings.

On a hot day in June 1892 he was driving an up goods train from Swindon and by Southall he was parched as only he could be so he brought his train to a stand on the up relief line, alongside the station's water column – with the Red Lion opposite, only a few paces away over the railings – and told his fireman to 'put the bag in' (fill the engine's water tank) while he 'went to church'. Naturally this played havoc with the train service and he was fined £1. And so it went on, fines and suspensions – entailing weeks without any money coming into the house for Catherine and the children – until during July and August 1899 he was absent so many times and for such long periods that he was dismissed with four weeks' notice and sent away with a reference of good character. Finally, he got a job working with the boilers and machinery of a stationary engine at Simmond's brewery in Reading and eventually became landlord of the King's Arms in Wallingford Street, Wantage, where he gave up his coal-burning soul in 1927, his last words being, to my grandfather, 'Fetch us a pint, Will.'

Evan Harry was born before his time – he ought to have been the driver of the 'Cheltenham Flyer' in the 1930s – in Pembrokeshire in February 1841 and joined the South Wales Railway at New Milford in 1855. New Milford was then the terminal for Cork and Waterford, a harbour station on the shore of Milford

Haven, reached by rail down a steep incline from Johnston station at the summit. Evan loved his pipe and his beer like anyone else but he was an especially happy man, a good dancer and a good singer too. He also loved to drive engines and was keen to go as fast as possible – he must have been a good mate to work with. In February 1871, when he had been a fireman for six years, he was on the pilot, his driver having gone off somewhere leaving him to do both jobs. The 9 p.m. up Irish goods drew out of the yard onto the bank and stood ready for the pilot to buffer up behind as 'banker'. The siding points were opened by the policeman and Evan drove out, rather too enthusiastically, crashed into the rear of the goods and de-railed some wagons. The Company thought this was only worth a reprimand and left it at that, not, apparently, making any inquiry into the driver's absence.

In December 1871 Evan rose a step to become an engine turner: a driver restricted to moving engines about the shed when they have finished their day's work or before they start their day, a grade below that of 3rd class engineman but in the wilds of west Wales somewhat flexibly employed. In March 1873, still as an engine turner, he was out on the main line, driving the bank engine and was returning 'light' from Johnston after assisting a train up the hill. Down he came at a cracking pace. He failed to stop at New Milford's distant signal which stood at 'Danger' and at which he was therefore bound to stop under the rules then applying, shot past the home signal at 'Danger' into a siding where a rake of wagons was standing and hit them so hard that the one at the far end cannoned off and disappeared with a loud splash into the dark waters of the Haven. That breach of half a dozen rules cost him £1 and in July he was promoted to 3rd class driver and sent to Cardiff.

He worked all kinds of lowly goods trains to and from collieries in the Valleys and in the anonymous dockland branches, always cheerful, never greatly concerned about such things as stop signals, and collecting fines and suspensions for collisions as easily as he made friends with the people living near the lineside where his train called to work. He was on one job with a colliery pick-up which took him down the main line to Llantrisant and then north into the hills, to Gellyrhaidd Junction, where the line to Gilfach Goch diverged from the Blackmill and Tondu line. Gellyrhaidd was a windswept place, high on the moors with only a solitary house in sight, a farm about 500 yds from the line. The signalman at the junction knew the family well and bought eggs and milk from them, so it was not long before Evan was going across to the house for food and spending half an hour or so in the kitchen, warming himself, while his fireman got on with shunting work. It was a cosy arrangement and worked well because it was not overdone but just after his birthday in February 1874, Evan was rostered on the Gilfach trip and a birthday party was arranged for him at the farm. He arrived at Gellyrhaidd with his best clothes and dancing shoes in a linen bag in the engine's tool box, backed his train into a siding and set off across the heather with his party clothes in one hand. The trouble arose because he was gone for five hours; other trains arrived, were unable to use the siding as they ought to have done, delays occurred; Authority discovered Evan's pleasant arrangements and Evan got the sack.

Undeterred and quite determined to be an engine driver he trekked to Newport where he persuaded the Monmouthshire Railway & Canal Company to take him on as a driver and he started work for them in April 1874. In September 1875 the MR&C was taken over by the Great Western and with it Evan Harry. There were no hard feelings; Evan carried on driving between Newport (Dock Street) and Coedygric Junction, Pontypool, until exactly two years after his re-entry into the Great Western he allowed his fireman to burn the engine's boiler whereupon the Great Western ejected him once more.

But Evan had what the Army at a later date was to call 'bags of initiative'. He really loved driving – the money was good too – so he looked around for another driving job. He needed a small railway, not professionally managed, a little, local line, glad of his expertise and not knowledgeable enough to ask searching questions. He hit on exactly the right place – the Malmesbury Railway, just over six miles long from the Great Western main line at Dauntsey, south-west of Swindon. The line was an independent company run by local businessmen although the Great Western had put money into it and supplied the engines and carriages. Evan knew that if he was hired it would be by a committee of grocers rather than railwaymen; what he supplied for references is not known but he boldly offered his cheerful services, was taken on and started driving when the line opened in December 1877. He could not have been happier. He was driving a Great Western engine on what was virtually his private railway with a pub at Dauntsey and a whole town full of pubs at Malmesbury where he was a personage – the Malmesbury Railway's driver with always a shilling or two to jingle in his pocket. In 1880 his private railway was formally absorbed into the Great Western which effortlessly digested him as well. Occasionally, over the years that followed, he would de-rail his engine or forget to oil some part so that a rod seized-up or fell off but now Authority at Swindon took a lenient view and even when his eyesight and hearing began to fade he was allowed to remain as branch driver until, aged nearly sixty-eight, he was asked to resign and take his pension. He retired reluctantly in January 1908 and died – brokenhearted perhaps – the following year.

Dishonesty did not always result in dismissal. The foreman at Llanelly shed in 1876 began a wages fiddle where he used his son to do work about the shed normally done by men. The men's wages were drawn and all concerned shared the proceeds. The foreman was sacked but appealed immediately and within the week had been reinstated and began driving on the Calne branch. Subsequent crashes into the blocks at Chippenham or Calne termini, parts of the engine breaking as a result of lack of oil, running out of steam on the 5½-mile-long branch were all treated leniently and he finally retired with his pension aged sixty-nine.

A man's fate seemed to depend on who he knew or before

which official of the Company he appeared; a driver, who was caught taking home a bundle of railway straw intended for cattle trucks, was taken to court, found guilty of the 'theft of a bundle of straw' and was dismissed from the service. A Swindon-based driver was ordered to Bristol to take his promotion to 1st class engineman on 4 March 1889. The man was fifty years old and refused to go on the ground that he was too old to take up express work. It was obligatory to take promotion and to go wherever you were sent – you could ask to be transferred home at the earliest possible moment or you might be lucky and find a man with whom you could do a swap but normally you had to go or face dismissal. This Swindon driver was allowed to remain in his 2nd class driving job but on 23 March he was again ordered to become a 1st class engineman, this time at Paddington for top link work. This so alarmed him that he went sick – so sick that he was removed to the County Asylum in Devizes where he suffered the hardships then inflicted on the mentally ill until July 1890 when he was pronounced cured. The Great Western took him back as an engine turner on Swindon shed. The engines he handled were usually in a state of 'undress', so to speak, off-duty, low in steam, the yard and shed were crowded with locomotives on which and under which men were working and a good deal of concentration and expertise was needed to do the job safely, attributes which our man, still nervous and depressed, did not have. For nine years he dragged unhappily on on 5 shillings a day, beyond retirement age, paying the occasional fine for moving an engine when a man was working underneath it – a very dangerous, easily fatal thing to do – forgetting to see if the tender's water scoop was retracted before moving the engine and thus ripping it off against the sleepers; he was earning 30 shillings or so each week, so a fine of 5 shillings was a great loss and hardship. He became more depressed and more withdrawn, ignored by most men – he was a 'cripple' driver who had refused the top link – noticed only when his feeble concentration went and he nearly killed someone. No one suggested that he retire and take his pension; he just kept coming to work out of habit and the fear of the emptiness of retirement.

The end came quickly and tragically. In April 1908, aged sixty-nine, he was caught trying to take home a small bag of coal with which to eke out the small supply he was able to buy with his meagre earnings. The hero of moral rectitude who apprehended his villainy threw the coal back on an engine's tender and reported him for theft. The case did not go to court as usual, but stayed with Mr Churchward, the Chief Locomotive and Carriage Superintendent, who probably thought he was being very liberal in not letting the matter take its usual course. Churchward was an engineer through and through – and a great one – but gentleness was the least of his virtues, indeed, his was what might safely be described as 'a blunt, outspoken' nature. He sentenced the old driver to a reduction in wages to 3 shillings a day and ordered that he retire at the end of the year. Had the case gone to court, the old man would undoubtedly have been found guilty of theft and dismissed automatically so Churchward probably felt he was being very fair but it was lack of money for basic essentials which had caused the trouble in the first place so that to reduce the wages still further was ridiculous. He had in fact sentenced the man to a fine of £16 8s and to a further seven months of working in misery for next to nothing. It was too much for the wretched man to bear. He handed in his notice when he left Churchward's office after the hearing and next morning was found drowned in the canal just outside the engine shed.

From 1849 the broad-gauge 'Flying Dutchman' was the pride and joy of the Great Western Railway, even when, from 1872, the line was predominantly standard gauge and Brunel's 7-ft gauge a resource-consuming nuisance. When the Midland Railway and, later, lesser companies, introduced corridor coaches and Pullman-car luxury with gas-light the 'Flying Dutchman' flew imperturbably on in defiance of the times, and very often its schedule too* – six wheeled, non-corridor, unheated, oil-lit

* See Appendix 3.

carriages behind Gooch 'Singles', magnificent to look upon but virtually unaltered since 1847. The Board did not want to spend money on modernising a doomed system but the Chairman, Sir Daniel Gooch, could not bring himself to break faith with Brunel and order its abolition – so it was kept running between Paddington and Penzance and between 1871 and 1888 twenty-four new broad-gauge engines were built to maintain the express services to the west. These were the 'Rover'-class engines, almost identical to the original, and now hopelessly under-powered, 1847 design except that the new engines had cabs and were turned out to look quite heroically beautiful. In June 1879, intense pressure from the General Manager, Mr Grierson, William Dean, Locomotive Superintendent, and the Divisional Superintendents forced George Tyrrell to sanction a relief, broad-gauge express to take the extreme overloading off the 'Flying Dutchman' which had become a very unreliable train from this cause. When Tyrrell became Superintendent of the Line in February 1864, economy was paramount; he was chosen by the Board because he was conservative and disliked speed and he promptly abolished all express trains* on the Great Western with the exception of the 'Flying Dutchman' and in 1869 he went so far as to abolish that too. Competition from the L&SWR and the relentlessly increasing demand for fast trains made him reinstate this, the Company's 'flagship', in 1871 but all other trains remained miserably slow. This new broad-gauge train, the first for seventeen years, was sheer recklessness as far as Tyrrell was concerned but he salvaged some decency from the situation by forbidding it to carry 3rd class passengers. It left Paddington at 3 p.m., ran to 'Flying Dutchman' timings and was immediately dubbed the 'Zulu' by Great Western men probably because at that time the British army was fighting the fierce, fast-running Zulu people and the epic events were daily described in the newspapers.

The 'Flying Dutchman' and the 'Zulu' were the fastest trains

---

* Express trains were those that averaged 40 mph inclusive of stops.

in the world and attracted a large traffic of passengers but they literally had to pay their money and take their chance. The magnificent, Gooch, 8-ft 'Singles' lost time if they were one carriage over their standard loading of five or if there was a strong headwind and if conditions allowed them to show how well they could run a carriage axle bearing would overheat and bring the train to a stand. Sometimes all worked perfectly and they would cruise superbly at 60 mph on level track.

George Tyrrell retired in June 1888, aged seventy-two, and was replaced by N. J. Burlinson, a young, energetic man; other old-hands retired and new men, keen to wake Brunel's railway from its long sleep, took over. Only one obstacle remained – Daniel Gooch, practically the sole reason for the continuation of the broad gauge. In May 1889 he told a meeting of shareholders that 'the abolition of the broad gauge cannot be long delayed'. It *was* a premonition of sorts because five months later, on 15 October, he died – the man who, with Isambard Kingdom Brunel and Charles Saunders, had been the driving force behind the broad gauge. There was nothing now to prevent its abolition but first, in June 1890, Burlinson introduced its swansong – the 'Cornishman' – the 10.15 a.m. from Paddington, faster than the 'Flying Dutchman', with new, bogie coaches and carrying 3rd class passengers. The carriages were built with standard-gauge bodies running on broad-gauge bogies and were often hauled by powerful, new, 7ft 8in. 'Singles' which were similarly convertible.

There were 213 route miles of broad-gauge track to be converted to standard, 4ft 8½in. gauge – what the Great Western had up till recently referred to disparagingly as 'narrow gauge', all of this between Exeter and Truro as well as miles of sidings at stations great and small between these places. Thirty-six miles of this was on modern, cross-sleepered track so a third rail was laid within the 7-ft gauge ready for when it was needed, leaving 177 miles of true, Brunellian 'baulk road', laid on the longitudinal sleepers, to be converted. Two days were all that was allowed for the job – 21 and 22 May 1892 – and so confident was the Company that this was sufficient time that they advertised beforehand that the 9 p.m. Paddington to Penzance mail of 22 May would proceed from Plymouth at 4.40 a.m. on the 23rd and this it did – dead on time.

Fifteen miles of sidings were laid on fields between Swindon Works and the embankment of the Midland & South Western Junction Railway to accommodate the redundant, broad-gauge engines and stock – there is still a scrapyard on this site, known as 'The Field' – and a nest of sidings totalling three miles in length was also laid at Bridgwater as a holding depot. Goods traffic west of Plymouth was suspended on the evening of Tuesday 17 May and freight for destinations between Exeter and Plymouth was suspended from 7.30 a.m. on the 18th after the last broad-gauge freight train to Plymouth, the 10.25 p.m. Paddington – 'The Tip' – had passed. After that the only goods traffic between Exeter and Truro were the engines with brake vans going down to bring back trains of broad-gauge carriages and wagons. Passenger trains continued to run, including the many specials needed to bring 3,400 permanent-way men from Bristol, Chester, New Milford, Paddington, Tondu and Weymouth to reinforce the local gangs and in all 4,200 men – twenty-four per mile – were distributed along the line. They brought their own rations with them, the Company supplying cooking facilities and an unlimited supply of the traditional and unexciting drink for all gauge-changers: oatmeal and water gruel. The man camped out in large tents, or in barns, goods sheds and station offices, the Chester men being posted to the Totnes area, the Welshmen to Falmouth. Their Inspectors and higher officials found lodgings in cottages in handy villages and all were received with such hospitality and enthusiasm that one Inspector commented: 'It was as if we were an army returning from a victorious campaign.'

At Paddington on 20 May, up broad-gauge trains arrived, were emptied and worked back immediately to Swindon for the scrapyard while engines for the last handful of broad-gauge down expresses stood on the shed roads for their final grooming at the hands of and under the supervision of a remarkable seventy-five-year-old cockney, a spry, little man, his face fringed around with a rope of grey beard under his ceremonial black bowler which marked the awfulness of the hour; the man was Charlie Weller, cheerful and active as ever in spite of the pain he now suffered from old injuries received at work. He had served the Great Western as a shed labourer-cum-messenger since Gooch took him on in 1838, had worked days and nights on end in those early days, helping to keep the railway going when they were virtually on their knees and drawing water from an old saw pit to keep the engines running. Over the years he had fractured his skull when he fell off an engine's framing, lost the sight of one eye when a piece of hot cinder fell in it while he was clearing out an ashpan, down in the pit, below the engine and twice had had his ribs crushed when he was accidentally squeezed between two engines' buffers. Fifty-four years on and he was still at work, writing happy poems about primroses or larks and pinning them up around the shed and now he was giving his all to send Sir Daniel's engines home in the best possible style.

Great Western took the 10.15 a.m. Paddington, the 'Cornishman', out of Paddington in a blaze of brass, a glitter of rivet heads, the 'Flying Dutchman' and the 'Zulu' left behind immaculate engines but when the very last broad-gauge engine backed onto the coaches of the very last down broad-gauge express it did so to an appreciative chorus of 'Ah!' and 'Oh!' from the assembled throng. Charlie Weller had kept the best till last, done the impossible and improved on perfection – *Bulkeley*, the last engine of an era, was the most highly polished of them all. *Bulkeley* took the 5 p.m. Paddington as far as Bristol where it waited for the up Mail from Penzance which it hauled back to Paddington on Saturday morning and then, in all its brassy glory, it ran down to Swindon for the scrap heap. Not one was spared.

The 5 p.m. Paddington continued westwards that Friday evening behind *Iron Duke* and was brought to a stand at Dawlish because the single-track section westwards to Teignmouth was occupied by the up Penzance Mail. When that train arrived at Dawlish it stopped and passengers in both trains joined hands across the six-foot way and sang 'Auld Lang Syne'.

At Swindon that Friday, freshly out-shopped eight-wheeled carriages, fully modernised with corridors, steam heating and even lavatories and a brand new Travelling Post Office eight-wheeler for the Plymouth 'Ocean Mail' traffic mingled with ancient, broad-gauge carriages and locomotives, their rods thrown up on their tenders, waiting to be pulled down into the scrapyard. Going west on the 'Flying Dutchman' that day *The Times* special reporter saw train after train going east, broad-gauge goods wagons, train after train, ancient designs dredged up from the backs of carriage sheds, which had never before been east of Plymouth; ugly old South Devon Railway tanks; handsome Bristol & Exeter Railway 4-2-4 tanks with driving wheels 8 ft 10 in. tall – the engine stock of the line to Penzance one might have thought – but at Plymouth the sidings were crammed with vehicles and engines all waiting to make that last, fateful journey to Swindon.

Plymouth North Road and the dock station at Millbay were crowded with excited sightseers as well as some unhappy drivers, the latter standing around with their firemen, disconsolate, carrying the lamps and tools off their old engines, waiting to take over their new-fangled, narrow-gauge machines, looking as worried as boys at a new school, wondering how they were going to cope. The 9 p.m. Mail from Paddington came into North Road behind a Great Western narrow-gauge engine, having travelled the South Western route from Exeter via Okehampton and Lydford and was the first narrow- or standard-gauge train to arrive. The mails were quickly unloaded and taken by galloping carts down to Millbay where the Great Western's splendid, twin-screw, steamer *Gazelle* of the Weymouth/Channel Islands service was waiting to receive them. The big, wickerwork hampers were loaded on board till she was stacked high in the waist and then she made way for Falmouth, calling at Fowey on the way to disembark the St Austell and Bodmin traffic.

The very last broad-gauge train of all was the 9.45 p.m. Penzance to Paddington, the up Mail, which arrived at Plymouth North Road at 1 a.m. on Saturday 21 May and left in a storm of cheering and flashing bangs as a fusillade of fog signals detonated beneath the engine's wheels. On board was the Chief Inspector of the Plymouth Division whose job was to make sure that all broad-gauge lines had been certified as clear of broad-gauge stock, to check all stations and sidings and then to issue the 'Last Broad Gauge Train' certificate to each station master. As the up Mail cleared each section and the certificates were issued the permanent-way men moved onto the track and by five o'clock, the Mail was clear of Exeter and not one broad-gauge vehicle was left in the West Country after forty-three years of their constant use.

The work of converting the gauge began as the sun rose on Saturday 21 May 1892. It was a glorious, spring day which encouraged spectators on every bridge and along the lineside fences. Preparations had begun days before; the ballast scraped away; every second transom holding the longitudinals to gauge had been cut to 4ft 8½in.-gauge length; all iron tie-rods, of which there were thousands, had either been cut to the new length or had had their threads greased to make it easy to dismantle when the time came; rails cut to the correct length had been laid around all curves – and there was virtually no straight track in Devon and Cornwall. The work consisted of removing the remaining tie-rods, cutting them to size, cutting all remaining transoms, slewing in one of the longitudinals and then re-assembling and re-ballasting. A gang of ten or twelve men with big crowbars levered in unison against the timbers and on the rare straights the job was simple enough – it was on the multitude of curves that the job became laborious in the extreme because the radii described by the rails of the 7-ft gauge track was greater than that described by the 4ft 8½in.-gauge rails around the same curve – hence the specially cut and pre-placed rails but if someone had not done his sums quite right and the new rail was in inch too long then that inch had to be cut – or rather hacked – off, there being no metal-cutting saws in those days. One man held a chisel to the rail by means of a hazel wand twisted round it so that he could hold it and yet keep his distance from the sledgehammer with which his mate walloped the chisel. It took thirty minutes to cut through a rail.

At the single-track Marley tunnel, west of Totnes, the roof began to cave in on the men as they worked while on the hilltop 100 ft above the rails a deep crevasse appeared. The roof stabilised and the intrepid labourers went back inside to work while others made arches of long lengths of bent rails, cut off the offending bulge and shored up the roof by jamming in their impromptu reinforcements – the tough rails, specially designed *not* to bend, being bent using the simple 'Jim Crow' device. The strata through which the tunnel lay had been weakened by the boring of a second tunnel alongside during 1891.

The 4,200 men worked sixteen hours a day, Saturday and Sunday, eating solid food before dawn and after dusk, drinking oatmeal and smoking their pipes during the day – towards which small luxury Mr Wills, the manufacturer of Bristol, had contributed 5 cwt or 2 oz per man. In spite of occasional landslides and the lack of any of the tools now considered essential, the tedious, laborious work of conversion was completed in thirty-two hours and without any mistakes. The first train over the new track was the up 'Cornishman', 11.10 a.m. off Penzance on 23 May which, in spite of official cautions to go slowly over the new track, arrived at Plymouth before time and arrived four minutes early at Paddington – just to show what the little, narrow-gauge engines could do.

The success of the conversion was due to remarkably well planned 'staff work' by the Chief Engineer, the aptly named Mr Trench, and the Plymouth Divisional Engineer, Mr Gibbons, but nothing would have happened without the amazing skill and physical endurance of the one pound a week labourers. *The Times* Special Correspondent wrote of them:

The men set to work with a cheerful good humour which cannot be too highly praised, the brisk energy they have shown throughout is worthy of the highest admiration though it must be confessed that this afternoon, now that the work is nearly over, some of them do look rather fagged – and after all, however fortifying a beverage oatmeal and water may be, sixteen hours' work on end is a very serious matter.

So Brunel's great railway – 'the finest work in England' he promised it to be – was slewed into history by the same brawny effort which had built it. When it was conceived the 7-ft gauge was far ahead of its time yet, paradoxically, Brunel was ten years too late in laying it out – the 'coal-cart' gauge and the reputation of George Stephenson were both too well established by 1840. Brunel envisaged high speed with comfort and stability all the way to New York via Great Western trains, hotels and ships and provided the basis for this with his 'billiard table road' while Gooch supplied the locomotives to realise the dream, for, if George Stephenson was the 'Father of Railways' then Daniel Gooch was the 'Father of Express Trains' and picked the right bunch of steel-nerved men to do the job. 'Wor Bill' Thompson's offer of 120 mph to Bristol from Paddington has only just been realised in 1980 yet it was the performance of Gooch's 1847 locomotives which moved him to make the offer and it was the timidity of the Directors that prevented him from achieving it. Brunel had given them a superb line; nothing else, they felt, was necessary. The great man went on to design the rest of his line to the west – his great ships – and the strains and worry he suffered through these fresh adventures caused his death at a relatively early age while the other pioneers lived long and comfortably to set the Great Western firmly in its corporate way, 'doing all things great and small with the immovability of Jove'. Without the Napoleonic energy of its great Engineer and with many other circumstances combining against it the Great Western almost went to sleep – but not quite. Under Tyrrell and Gooch the Severn tunnel was built, the longest underwater tunnel in the world, a truly gigantic achievement, engineered by one of Brunel's hand-picked assistants, Charles Richardson, and carried out by thousands of the bravest working men in the land.

Luckily the Great Western was blessed with many gallant spirits intent on modernising and returning Brunel's line to its old position of pre-eminence. They had to sweep away his 7-ft gauge but they still had the Brunellian bequest of morale, a sense of being unique – the best – and as a new century dawned that feeling became a reality.

APPENDIX ONE

Gooch's Letter of Application to Brunel, 1837

Manchester & Leeds Railway Office,
Rochdale

July 18th 1837

I.K. Brunel Esqre

Dear Sir,
I have just been informed it is your intention to erect an Engine Manufactory at or near Bristol and that you wish to engage a person as manager. I take the earliest opportunity of offering my services for the situation.

I have until the last two months been constantly engaged in Engine Building and have worked in each branch of the business, but principally at Locomotive Engine Work. The first three years of my time I was with Mr Humphrey at The Tredegar Iron Works, Monmouthshire, I left him to go to Mr R. Stephenson and was at the Vulcan Foundry twelve months when I obtained leave from Mr Stephenson to go down to Mr Stirling of the Dundee Foundry Co., Dundee – to get a knowledge of Steam boat work. I remained with him twelve months and returned to Mr Stephenson's works at Newcastle where I remained until last October, when I left having had an offer from a party in Newcastle to take the management of a Locomotive Manufactory which they intended erecting – but which owing to some unavoidable circumstances they have now given up the idea of proceeding with – and we have countermanded the orders for Machinery.

This has left me without a Situation and I am anxious to engage myself to some company where I will have the management of the building of Engines. At present I am with my brother on the Manchester and Leeds line where I have employment until I meet with something more suitible.

I will be glad to refer you to any of the aforementioned places – for testemonial.

I trust you approve of my application. I shall be glad to hear from you stating the salary and any other information you may think necessary.

I am, sir,

Yours obediently

Dan. I. Gooch

APPENDIX TWO

Great Western Railway

INSTRUCTIONS AS TO DISTINCTIVE GREAT WESTERN
ENGINE HEAD LIGHTS, HEAD MARKS, AND TARGETS,
ANNOUNCING SPECIAL TRAINS FOLLOWING, TO BE
USED ON THE GREAT WESTERN LINE (February 1883)

Clause 1.

HEAD LIGHTS AND HEAD MARKS.
REGULAR PASSENGER AND GOODS TRAINS.

BY DAY —An Ordinary Lamp under the Chimney,
unlighted.
BY NIGHT.—Excepting in the cases referred to in
Clauses 2 and 3 all Regular Trains must carry One
White Light under the Chimney, thus—

Clause 2.

"RELIEF LINES" BETWEEN LONDON AND SLOUGH.

BY NIGHT.—The Engines of all Regular Trains
running over the "Relief Lines" between London
and Slough must carry Two White Head Lights,
one under the other, thus—
BY DAY.—Two Lamps in the same position,
unlighted.

Clause 3.

REGULAR EXPRESS Goods, Cattle and Market Trains.

Between Paddington and Penzance (on Main
Line), Didcot and Wolverhampton (via
Banbury), Swindon to New Milford,
Chippenham and Weymouth, Gloucester
and Hereford.
BY DAY.—A White Diamond painted on a Black
ground on the Head lamp, fixed in the centre of the
Buffer plank, and showing to the front, thus—

BY NIGHT.—Two White Lights, thus—

Note.—These Trains when travelling over the "Relief Lines" between Slough and London, will use the ordinary "Relief Line" Head Lights and Head Marks, as shown in Clause 2.

Between Oxford and Wolverhampton (via West Midland), Worcester to Swansea, via Pontypool Road and Aberdare; Shrewsbury and Hereford, and the line north of Wolverhampton.

BY NIGHT.—One White Light over right-hand Buffer, and one Green Light over left-hand Buffer, thus—

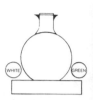

BY DAY.—One unlighted Lamp over right-hand Buffer, and one Lamp with White Diamond showing to the front over left-hand Buffer, thus—

Clause 4.

SPECIAL PASSENGER, GOODS, OR MINERAL TRAINS, WILL CARRY

BY DAY.—The Letter **S** painted in Red on a White Ground on the Head Lamp and showing to the front, thus—

BY NIGHT.—One **Green** Head Light at the foot of the Chimney, thus—

Note.—When Special Trains are travelling over the "Relief Lines" between London and Slough at night, the Engines must carry one White Light under the chimney and a Green Light in the centre of the Buffer plank, thus—

Clause 5.

SPECIAL FISH, PARCELS, MEAT, NEW POTATO, OR BROCCOLI TRAINS, WILL CARRY

BY DAY.—Two Lamps, one under the Chimney with the letter S, the other in the middle of the Buffer plank with a White Diamond painted on Black ground, thus—

BY NIGHT.—One Green Light under the Chimney, and one White Light in the middle of Buffer plank, thus—

> NOTE.—Special Trains, when travelling of the "Relief Line," between Slough and London, will use the ordinary "Relief Line" Head Lights and Head Marks as shown in Clause 2. Between Dorchester and Weymouth all Great Western Specials carry one White Light in the centre of the Buffer plank, and one Green Light at the foot of the chimney.

Signalmen and all others concerned must see that Trains having these Head marks and Head lights shall take precedence of, and pass all other Goods and Mineral Trains they may overtake on the road; and each Train so distinguished when running over lines where Block Telegraph is in use must be signalled forward in accordance with the Rule "Shunt for Fast Train" of the Standard Block Telegraph Regulations, and on parts of the line where the Block Telegraph is not in use, between each principal Station by means of the ordinary speaking instrument, so that the Stations in advance may be prepared with a clear road for these Trains. The object of the distinguishing Signals on the Engines is to ensure prompt and sufficient advice being given to Stations in advance in order that the Special trains may not be delayed.

Clause 6.

Engine Head Lamps that are not actually in use in compliance with the instructions contained herein must not be carried in front of the Engine.

TARGETS.

Clause 7.

TARGETTING TRAINS PRECEDING SPECIAL TRAINS.

SPECIAL PASSENGER TRAINS.

A Red Target, Double Disc, or extra Tail Lamp *by day* and the Double Red Lamps *by night* must be attached to the rear of the preceding Train except as provided for in the following clause.

DIVIDED PASSENGER TRAINS.

When it is necessary to divide a Passenger Train by running a Special Train in front of a **late** Ordinary Train, the Special Train will take the time of the Ordinary Train, and be distinguished by carrying a Special Train Head mark or light in front (as shewn in Clause 4), and a Double Disc by day, or Double Red Lamps by night at the rear of the Train; *the second or ordinary* portion of the Train to carry ordinary Head and Tail Lamps.

SPECIAL GOODS AND MINERAL TRAINS ON DOUBLE LINES.

On Double Lines, when Special Goods or Mineral Trains have to be run without previous notice, the preceding Train **must not** be targetted **except** between Exeter and Penzance, where the preceding Train must carry the tail-signals prescribed below:—

Special Passenger ⎰ Double Red Disc...................................By day.
Train to follow ⎱ Double Red Lamps...............................By night.
Special Goods ⎰ Double Disc, one Red, one Green..........By day.
Train to follow ⎱ Double Lamps, one Red and one Green By night.

SPECIAL PASSENGER OR GOODS TRAINS RUN ON SINGLE LINES.

In *all* cases of Special Passenger or Goods Trains having to be run over a single Line (except between Exeter and Penzance provided for in preceding clause) the Double Red Targets to indicate "Special to Follow" *must be* attached to the train preceding such Special Train.

Clause
8.

NOTICE OF SPECIAL GOODS TRAINS.

A written notice of Special Goods Trains must be given whenever possible; in cases, however, of such Trains having to run at short notice, and no written notice being possible, they must be telegraphed from the starting point, to the principal stations in advance.

NOTE.—This Circular supersedes all previous Circulars on the subject.

G. N. TYRRELL,

February, 1883,   *Superintendent of the Line.*

An acknowledgement of the receipt hereof to be obtained from Station Masters, Signalmen, Guards, and others by the Head of Department.

Report on the 'Flying Dutchman'
Letter from William Dean to Daniel Gooch, 8 May 1879

My Dear Sir Daniel,

In reply to yours of 7th inst. I fear the hot boxes are caused partly by the special grease we have been making for the 'Dutchman' being too rich in quality i.e. containing too high a proportion of tallow and palm oil. We are now making some of a different mixture and hope to get a better result. I will give the matter close attention until we overcome the difficulty.

On some days the rain has been exceedingly heavy and delays have occurred at stations; time has also been lost in running but this cannot well be avoided when the load is excessive as the speed is high and the engines cannot do much more than keep time even with average loads. The proposed new trains up and down may relieve this train a little and so help us. I do not think there will be much to complain of when we have got rid of the hot boxes.

William Dean

Statement showing the working of the 8.35 a.m. express ('Flying Dutchman') from Plymouth to Paddington for one month ending 5 May 1897

April	Min. late Pdn.	Remarks
5	2	
7	53	Stopped 12 minutes at Twyford and 13 at Slough to cool hot boxes and then ran reduced speed to avoid overheating the axles again.
8	3	
9	36	3 minutes outside Kingsbridge Rd. waiting down train.

	Min. late	
April	Pdn.	*Remarks*

4 min. at Newton attaching coaches from branch train which was late. 2 minutes at Dawlish, 1 at Exeter, 2 at Taunton examining tickets. 8 at Bristol transferring luggage and detaching coach with hot box. 11 minutes lost by engine Dawlish–Paddington. Heavy train.

10   21   5 minutes lost at Newton waiting branch (Kingswear) train and attaching a coach therefrom. 2 lost Bristol, 2 at Swindon. 11 lost by engine Plymouth–Swindon. Heavy train and wet rail.

12   12   2 lost at Newton. 2 lost Exeter detaching coach with hot box. 2 at Bristol seating passengers. 5 lost by engine Dawlish–Swindon.

14   19   19 lost by engine, snow storm and strong wind.

15   20   1 minute lost Kingsbridge Rd. 1 lost at Newton. 1 at Teignmouth. 2 at Taunton washing out hot box on Compo 207W. Stopped at Langley to cool hot box on Van 121W.

16   31   4 minutes lost Bristol attaching extra coach, train full. 5 lost at Swindon collecting excess fare from passenger. 21 lost at Reading washing out hot box on Compo.

17   5   5 minutes lost by engine.

18   8   Time lost by engine, one extra coach and strong wind.

19   19   3 lost Kingsbridge Rd, down train late off single line. 3 lost at Newton attaching/detaching coaches. 2 lost Swindon. Engine lost 8 minutes Plymouth–Paddington. Very strong side wind.

21   46   Excessively heavy train. Delayed at all stations where it called, Dawlish to Paddington in finding seats for passengers, stowing luggage, collecting tickets and excess fares. Engines lost 24 minutes. Nine vehicles instead of five.

22   88   22 minutes lost by engine Plymouth–Swindon (two vans of gold bullion). Stopped at Maidenhead, Slough and Southall to wash out hot boxes.

23   7   7 minutes over at Bristol detaching Compo with hot box.

April	Min. late Pdn.	Remarks
24		TIME
25	6	Delayed through Paddington yard, preceding train late.
26	45	Engine broke connecting rod at Kingsbridge Rd. Stopped at Taplow to wash out hot boxes on coach and van.
28	67	Engine out of order at Uffington – something wrong with injector feed pipe. Detained at Bristol to detach hot box. Engine lost time throughout and stopped for water at Slough.
29	60	Delay at Taunton detaching coach with hot box. Bristol waiting assistant engine and taking coal and water. Stopped at Southall to wash out three hot boxes.
30	15	8 minutes lost at Newton waiting the branch and attaching coach. 2 lost at Taunton, 3 lost at Bristol attaching extra coach, train full, no room for passengers.

May		
1	12	4 lost at Newton (branch and attatch coaches). Engine lost 6 minutes Plymouth–Bristol. Station work lost 1 minute at Taunton, 1 at Bristol.
2	2	
3	22	4 lost at Teignmouth crossing down goods. 3 lost at Swindon greasing axles. Stopped at Langley to wash out hot box on Compo 311W.
5	49	Started 2 minutes late waiting mail bags. 2 lost Newton (branch) 2 lost at Exeter, 3 lost at Taunton, 6 lost at Bristol transferring mail and detaching mail van. 4 lost at Bath finding room for luggage, 3 lost at Swindon washing out hot box and greasing. 15 lost at West Drayton cooling hot boxes on Compo and van.

Statement showing the working of the 11.45 a.m. express ('Flying Dutchman') *from Paddington to Plymouth for one month ending 5 June 1879*

May	Min. late Plym.	Remarks
5	4	2 lost by engine London to Swindon. 1 lost at Bath. Taunton.
7	RT	
8	35	Yatton, injector not working. Durston brake rod on Compo 305W broke.
9	59	Delay at all stations. Heavy East traffic. Engine lost 27 minutes London to Exeter. Very heavy train.
10	90	Delay all stations. Heavy Easter traffic. Engine lost 38 minutes Paddington to Newton Abbott. Double load.
12	14	14 minutes lost by engine Bristol to Exeter. Heavy snowstorm.
14	5	
15	RT	
16	5	
17	3	
18	RT	

19, 21, 22, 23: RT

24	3	

25, 26, 28, 29, 30: RT

June

1	18	12 minutes at Wantage Road washing out hot box. 16 minutes at Taunton washing out hot box.

2, 3, 5: RT

APPENDIX FOUR

Detailed Explanation of Plates 20–2

PLATE 20: The view westwards seen from a signal post at the west end of Swindon station about 1880. The route to Bristol is ahead, that to Gloucester curves to the right, the locomotive works is in the v of the junction, the carriage work on the downside of the Bristol line. The track is laid for mixed gauge so that narrow- and broad-gauge trains can pass. The left-hand rail (in the direction of running) was common to both gauges so that vehicles of both sorts could come close alongside a platform but problems arose where the track forked left to form a 'loop' around the back of an 'island' platform. In such a situation, if the common rail remained on the left then a narrow-gauge vehicle would arrive 27½ in. away from the platform edge. The common rail had therefore to change sides and become the right-hand rail whilst forming the loop line. To do this the train first passed the facing points onto the loop and then came to a 'fixed' point on the right. This was like a point which has had the movable blade removed to leave a narrow gap between it and the rail for 'straight-on' running. Opposite the fixed point, close to the narrow-gauge rail was a guide rail. The flanges of broad-gauge wheels passed this apparatus unhindered but the right-hand flange on narrow-gauge wheels was caught by the guide rail and forced hard to the right thus dragging the left-hand wheel sideways – it ran for a few inches on its flange on a flat, iron plate – until it re-located on the rail of the fixed point and it was thus diverted and moved across to the right within the confines of the broad gauge until it came against the platform edge and the right-hand rail was then the common rail. The system was introduced at Gloucester in 1847 when it was condemned as 'dangerous and impractical' by the Board of Trade though at the same time it was passed for public use subject to a speed limit of 8 mph which condition was applied to all subsequent installations. For all its dangerous impracticality the system was the cause of only one accident – at Bathampton in 1881.

PLATE 21: The common rail is re-crossing to the left as the tracks leave the island platform loop at Swindon. The open, fixed point is facing the camera, in the wooden crossing with the vital guide rail opposite, also in the wooden crossing, just in front of the men with barrows.

PLATE 22 shows in detail the practice of running signal wires overhead. This was the solution forced on the engineers in many locations where 'modern' signalling was added to existing, broad-gauge layouts. The problem was that broad-gauge rails lay not on cross sleepers but on longitudinal baulks and therefore there were no spaces beneath the wires through which the bunches of signal wires could pass from one side of the line to the other. Newton Abbott, Exeter, Didcot and the smaller installation at Lydney were equipped with overhead wires. At very small places, such as Waltham, only one or two wires required to cross the tracks and these could be strung at ground-level and cross the tracks through channels cut in the longitudinals. The brick building is the 'GWR Medical Fund Swimming Bath', thoughtfully placed at the edge of the path up from the sooty engine shed and the white house on the extreme right is a cunningly placed tavern, just right for home-going enginemen, standing on the bank of the Wilts & Berks canal which passes under the line here. Its door stands invitingly open but the cautious man would be wary of being seen entering or leaving the place – even if he was off duty.

INDEX